LEADING IMPROVEMENT IN
SCHOOL COMMUNITY WELLBEING

DONNA CROSS
LEANNE LESTER

amba
press

Published in 2025 by Amba Press, Melbourne, Australia
www.ambapress.com.au

First published in 2023 by ACER Press, an imprint of Australian Council for Educational Research Ltd

© Donna Cross and Leanne Lester 2025

This book is copyright. All rights reserved. Except under the conditions described in the *Copyright Act 1968* of Australia and subsequent amendments, and any exceptions permitted under the current statutory licence scheme administered by Copyright Agency (www.copyright.com.au), no part of this publication may be reproduced, stored in a retrieval system, transmitted, broadcast or communicated in any form or by any means, optical, digital, electronic, mechanical, photocopying, recording or otherwise, without the written permission of the publisher.

Edited by Shaneen Goodwin
Cover design, text design and typesetting by Nada Backovic

Paperback ISBN 9781923569164
ePub ISBN 9781923569171

A catalogue record for this book is available from the National Library of Australia.

Foreword

> *Research is revealing the powerful impact that school leadership teams can have in improving the quality of teaching and learning. Effective leaders create cultures of high expectations, provide clarity about what teachers are to teach and students are to learn, establish strong professional learning communities and lead ongoing efforts to improve teaching practices. (Masters 2012)*

School leadership is an increasingly complex, highly demanding role. School leaders are accountable for a broad range of factors and outcomes and to a wide array of stakeholders. In establishing short- and long-term goals for improving outcomes for students, school leaders must turn their minds not only to performance indicators and targets but to the methods, approaches and strategies through which those targets can be achieved.

Research tells us that schools and school systems that embrace evidence-based practice models are those most likely to achieve their goals of improving outcomes for young people. It also tells us that it is school leaders who play a critical role in identifying, implementing, embedding and leading evidence-based practice.

The 'High impact strategies for school leaders' series is designed as a resource for those busy school leaders whose ultimate aim is to improve outcomes for all learners. Each book in the series, focusing on a different domain within the school environment, unpacks for school leaders the ways high-impact strategies and practices can be applied to achieve improvement goals. Written by highly regarded experts in their fields, the series seeks to focus attention on the role of school leaders in driving the processes that result in effective school and classroom practice and improved outcomes for students and help them navigate through the dizzying array of information about 'what works' and what doesn't.

In *Leading improvement in school community wellbeing*, behavioural scientist and Emeritus Professor Donna Cross, and epidemiologist and biostatistician Dr Leanne Lester, highlight the role of principals and other school-based leaders in leading improvement in wellbeing outcomes. Cross and Lester present a range of evidenced-informed practices that can be used as a focus for teacher professional learning and school improvement, aligning each of these with high-impact whole-school strategies.

Through their work with the University of Western Australia and Telethon Kids, Cross and Lester have a wealth of experience and knowledge in the strategies and practices that lead to long-lasting and impactful change in student and teacher wellbeing. *Leading improvement in school community wellbeing* provides research evidence and practical tools to support 7 key wellbeing practices in schools, involving school climate; students' wellbeing, engagement and agency; policies and procedures; engagement with parents; curriculum activities; school physical environment; and staff wellbeing and professional capacity. In addition, an introductory chapter unpacks the importance of assessing the current situation in individual school contexts before embarking on actions for improvement.

Cross and Lester draw on some of their own well-received research and the work of other educational authorities in constructing the set of 7 high-impact wellbeing practices that shape this book. Together, these provide an effective framework for schools and school leaders to strengthen their wellbeing actions and subsequent student, teacher and community outcomes.

CONTENTS

Foreword		iii
Acknowledgements		vii
Introduction		1
Part 1:	**WHAT'S HAPPENING?**	11
	Assess the school community's wellbeing strengths and needs to determine actions needed to improve staff and student wellbeing	
Chapter 1:	Staff wellbeing is critical for student wellbeing	13
Chapter 2:	Assessing student wellbeing strengths and needs	47
Part 2:	**WHAT'S NEEDED?**	71
	Actions for continuous improvement for school community wellbeing	
Chapter 3:	Taking school community wellbeing from good to great: getting the climate right	73
Chapter 4:	Teacher relationships and classroom practices to build student wellbeing	99
Chapter 5:	Enabling student voice and participation for wellbeing: nothing about me without me	123
Chapter 6:	Organising the school for student wellbeing: roles and structures	145
Chapter 7:	The third teacher: the school physical environment and wellbeing	169
Part 3:	**WHAT'S NEXT?**	191
	Steps to effectively implement wellbeing actions needed to respond to staff and student strengths and needs	
Chapter 8:	Reviewing and renewing school wellbeing: pathways to make it happen	193

ACKNOWLEDGEMENTS

Donna Cross

> I want to acknowledge the years of encouragement and love my parents, Pat and Don, gave me to be as healthy as possible and to work hard to help others experience the same. To my husband, Evan, and my children, Will and Sarah, who keep me strong and true – thank you for your love and patience. Thanks also to Emma Charlton and Sarah Falconer for their help identifying evidence support.

Leanne Lester

> I would like to thank my family for their support, their animated discussions of research findings and their ability to make me laugh. Dave, Noah, Reuben, Joey and Anri – you are much loved and appreciated. I would also like to acknowledge the schools and wellbeing teams who were involved in the case studies and generously gave their time.

Introduction

The promotion of and support for students' wellbeing has long been identified as a key challenge in schools, with John Dewey (1907: 19) stating over a hundred years ago, 'What the best and wisest parent wants for his own child, that must the community want for all its children. Any other ideal for our schools is narrow and unlovely; acted upon, it destroys our democracy.'

However, only within the last 2 decades has the Australian Department of Education (Department of Education 2001) incorporated health and wellbeing policy to its model of academic care and education. Since then, a steady sequence of national initiatives such as *Safe and supported: the national framework for protecting Australia's children 2021–2031* (the national framework) (Commonwealth of Australia [Department of Social Services] 2021), the Australian Curriculum's inclusion of *Personal and Social Capability* (ACARA 2019) and the release of the *Australian Student Wellbeing Framework* (ESA 2018) have prioritised the importance of achieving a shared vision of physical and emotional safety and wellbeing for all students in all Australian schools. Similarly, key health and education organisations such as the OECD, WHO, UNICEF and UNESCO have encouraged policymakers in education, school staff and families to ensure students achieve their wellbeing potential.

These national and international health and education policy initiatives as well as substantial and growing empirical evidence underscore the critical impact the school setting has on school students' wellbeing. Further, the impacts of the COVID-19 pandemic and other natural disasters, such as floods and fires in Australia, have required a renewed focus on social and emotional wellbeing across the community and particularly in schools.

What do we mean by school wellbeing?

While there is almost unanimous agreement that wellbeing is important, there is very little agreement nationally and internationally about how to define it. Terms like 'pastoral care' and 'school wellbeing' along with some other terms like 'social and emotional wellbeing', 'welfare', 'school guidance', 'behaviour management' and 'mental health' have become almost interchangeable as they are used in schools to describe policies and practices to improve the school community's wellbeing.

Many schools' leadership teams have chosen to call their 'pastoral care program' their 'school wellbeing program', arguing that 'wellbeing' better describes the strengths-based outcomes of school policies and proactive practices for the school community. Further, the term 'pastoral care' can carry different meanings in a school community and is sometimes not well understood, suggesting it has had something to do with farming or has religious connotations. The term 'pastoral care' is used by some school leadership teams to suggest a deficit focus rather than emphasising students' strengths.

In this book, we define 'school wellbeing actions' (including policies, practices, procedures and programs) as 'all the actions taken by a school to support school community members – especially the staff and students – to build their strength and capacity to be happy and healthy now and into the future and to have the skills and ability to respond effectively to change and unpredictability'. These wellbeing actions include positive universal or school population-level actions for all students, actions for students identified as at risk of developing difficulties and actions for students experiencing difficulties. This definition is based on the OECD (2017) and AIHW (2009) definitions of school wellbeing policies and practices. Importantly, a definition of student wellbeing needs to reflect the social (interpersonal) and emotional (intrapersonal) capabilities of students. The simplest and most subjective wellbeing definition in regular use is 'feeling well, functioning well and feeling connected'. The definition of wellbeing is discussed in more detail when considering how to measure staff and student wellbeing in Chapters 1 and 2.

High-functioning schools ensure their wellbeing actions are an integrated, whole-school, evidence-based and coordinated strategy led by a trained wellbeing leadership team who benchmark, monitor and assess the impact of these actions on the wellbeing of their whole school community, particularly their staff and students (Lang 1999; Watkins 2004; Wylie 2005; Popovic 2002; Lodge 2006; Watkins 1999).

High-impact school wellbeing programs are much more than complementary practices developed through fragmented activities; instead they inextricably and holistically embed student wellbeing and academic outcomes formally and informally in the whole school through teacher pedagogy, curriculum teaching, the social and physical environment and organisation of the school – to support staff and meet students' personal, social and academic needs (Chittenden 2002). The evidence is clear that a whole-school approach is critical to improve wellbeing and academic outcomes. From this perspective, the wellbeing of the school community is 'everyone's business' that requires committed visible leadership and an explicit goal in the school's vision and mission to ensure it is prioritised.

These high-impact wellbeing programs have school leaders who ensure school wellbeing actions are determined with input from the school community (especially students) to increase their relevance, ownership and engagement and to build common understandings about what the school's wellbeing program does and does not include. In this environment, the school community can understand its roles, responsibilities and expectations related to improving its wellbeing – this clarity in turn breeds commitment.

What is the role of school leadership in improving wellbeing outcomes?

Not surprisingly, significant evidence shows the actions of the principal and other members of the school leadership team directly influence the wellbeing of the school community. This influence is primarily through the school climate or culture as a result of their leadership style, building social capital or trust within the school, encouraging and enabling quality relationships (Powell and Graham 2017) and by operationalising the vision, goals and mission of the school.

A meta-analysis (Robinson et al. 2007) measuring the impact of school leadership on student outcomes (including wellbeing) found school leaders most significantly influence student and staff wellbeing by:

> promoting and participating in teacher learning and development

> enhancing the quality of teaching and curriculum planning, coordination and evaluation

> establishing goals and expectations

> providing strategic resourcing

> sustaining an orderly and supportive environment.

This meta-analysis found that the commitment of the principal and leadership team to 'promoting and participating in teacher learning and development' had the greatest effect on student outcomes, with nearly twice the impact of the other 4 influences. While this active involvement in promoting staff learning and development demonstrates the school leadership's interest in improving wellbeing outcomes, it also intensifies the school leadership's appreciation of the issues and challenges teaching staff are experiencing and the support needed to address these (Robinson et al. 2007).

While it is critical for schools to be safe, proactive, preventative and caring to maximise students' wellbeing and learning, other high-impact practices include having clear behavioural expectations and policies, providing minimal disruption to teaching, a clear triage and proactive actions to resolve wellbeing issues effectively and, importantly, protecting the wellbeing of teachers.

What wellbeing goals should school leaders be targeting?

High-impact (evidence-based) and embedded school wellbeing practices can optimise students' social, emotional, physical, spiritual and cognitive functioning and capabilities and achievement. The reverse is also true: students' academic achievement and other capabilities can influence their wellbeing. Through this reciprocal relationship and school staff's sustained engagement and relationships with students, there is significant opportunity for school staff to promote the wellbeing of students, staff and other members of the school community.

High-impact leadership teams systematically embed wellbeing at the whole-school level, that is within the school budget, policies, structures, organisation, social climate, curriculum and pedagogy, family and community partnerships and the school's physical environment. They ensure wellbeing practices are not fragmented, and focus on prevention as well as higher risk students, with clear policy and practice direction, based on quality school-level evidence (Powell and Graham 2017; Victorian Auditor-General 2010). Moreover, they ensure there is quality evidence-based professional development and support for wellbeing leaders and staff to ensure the effective and systematic implementation of wellbeing practices by all staff. These school leaders and staff also clearly understand their whole school- and classroom-level wellbeing responsibilities within well-defined role descriptions.

Committed wellbeing leadership also addresses the growing tension within schools to provide sufficient resources to implement the full continuum of whole-school wellbeing practices from promotion, protection and prevention, through to early intervention for higher risk students and targeted interventions for students experiencing difficulties, such as depression, drug abuse and bullying (Short 2016). With limited wellbeing resources and increasing numbers of students with complex needs, especially in the wake of COVID-19 and other recent natural disasters, school leadership teams may find their wellbeing and allied health team operating only in crisis mode – with all wellbeing resources used to respond to wellbeing problems rather than also upstream universal wellbeing promotion, protection and prevention actions.

Using scarce resources well

To address wellbeing resourcing challenges, visible wellbeing leadership is needed to review and realign resources and staff effort to meet the unique context and strengths and needs of the school community. This means allocating resources for wellbeing based on school mapping and identifying current school actions to be maintained, stopped, modified or added. A strategic and systematic review process based on quality data collected from students and the school community helps school wellbeing teams to move beyond operating their wellbeing program based on the 'vibe' or feel of the school. These data also help leaders to better understand staff capacity to deliver effective wellbeing practices to meet the identified needs and to understand the impact of their school's current wellbeing activities.

Leading improvement in school wellbeing

Each chapter in this book describes evidence-based, high-impact actions found to positively influence the social and emotional wellbeing of the whole school community. The chapters are organised to prompt school leaders and the school community to reflect on 'what's happening' by assessing staff and student social and emotional wellbeing and then using insight from these student and staff wellbeing data to determine 'what's needed' in their school, in terms of high-impact actions to improve students' and other members of the school community's wellbeing. These high-impact actions can be used to improve school climate, teacher relationships and classroom practices, student participation and agency, wellbeing-promoting structures and organisation and the school's physical environment.

The final chapter of this book helps school leaders and their school community to decide 'what's next' as they consider how they are implementing and sustaining high-impact actions. This section supports school improvement processes to plan for, select, support, monitor and embed high-impact wellbeing actions.

Figure i. Leadership Implementation plan for high-impact practices for school community wellbeing

Figure i provides a summary framework of school wellbeing improvement processes and actions described in this book – with visible wellbeing leadership at the core. As shown in this figure and described above, to ensure the school improvement decision-making process is meaningful, it needs to be context based, involving the 'consumers', using student and teacher wellbeing data to inform decisions about what practices need to be implemented. Each of the high-impact actions – the 'what' described in this book – sit in the 3 inner rings of Figure i: committed visible leadership, staff wellbeing improvement, student wellbeing improvement, student participation and agency, wellbeing-promoting structures and organisation, school's physical environment, teacher relationships and classroom practice and school climate.

In addition to the implementation process shown in the 3 inner rings of Figure i, each step of the 8-step implementation process described in the outer circle is designed to help schools systematically assess and address their staff and students' wellbeing strengths, needs and opportunities and to help the school community to decide on, build capacity for and continue to implement the high-impact practices needed – how often, with whom, at what intensity and in what ways – while ensuring the school community remains informed. The 8 steps are:

1. Establish a dedicated wellbeing leadership team to drive implementation.
2. Review and take action to support staff wellbeing.
3. Collect and review student wellbeing outcomes.
4. Use data to assess wellbeing policy, practice and procedure.
5. Decide on wellbeing actions to stop, start, improve and keep.
6. Delineate staff wellbeing roles and responsibilities, and school structures and procedures.
7. Staff reflect on wellbeing practice through professional learning and mentoring.
8. Communicate progress and provide resources for monitoring and review.

While it can be challenging for school leaders to implement a wellbeing improvement plan, without leaders' highly visible commitment and the active involvement of the whole school, the effectiveness of any actions to improve student wellbeing will be significantly diminished – no matter what evidence exists about the usefulness of these actions.

Committed and visible school leadership is the most critical driver of high-impact actions to improve student and staff wellbeing.

References

ACARA (Australian Curriculum Assessment and Reporting Authority) (2019) *Personal and Social Capability (Version 8.4)*, ACARA website, accessed 17 January 2023. https://www.australiancurriculum.edu.au/f-10-curriculum/general-capabilities/personal-and-social-capability/

AIHW (Australian Institute of Health and Welfare) (2009) *A picture of Australia's children*, AIHW, Canberra.

Chittenden AHR (2002) 'A pastoral care teacher's theory of action, interactive thinking and effective teaching practice', *Pastoral Care in Education*; 20(1):3–10.

Commonwealth of Australia (Department of Social Services) (2021) *Safe and supported: the national framework for protecting Australia's children 2021–2031* (the national framework), Commonwealth of Australia, accessed 14 March 2023. https://www.dss.gov.au/sites/default/files/documents/12_2021/dess5016-national-framework-protecting-childrenaccessible.pdf

Department of Education (2001) 'Pathways to health and well-being in schools: A focus paper 2001', Department of Education.

Dewey J (1915) *The school and society*, Revised edn., The University of Chicago Press, Chicago, Ill.

ESA (Education Services Australia) (2018) *Australian Student Wellbeing Framework*, Education Council, Carlton South, VIC, accessed 17 January 2023. https://studentwellbeinghub.edu.au/educators/framework

Lang P (1999) 'Counselling, counselling skills and encouraging pupils to talk: clarifying and addressing confusion', *British Journal of Guidance & Counselling,* 27(1):23–33.

Lodge C (2006) 'Beyond the head of year', *Pastoral Care in Education*, 24(1):4–9.

OECD (2017) *Education at a glance 2017: OECD indicators*, OECD Publishing, Paris.

Popovic N (2002) 'An outline of a new model of personal education', *Pastoral Care in Education*, 20(3):12–20.

Powell MA, Graham A (2017) 'Wellbeing in schools: examining the policy–practice nexus', *Australian Educational Researcher*, 44(2):21–31.

Robinson VM, Hohepa M, Lloyd C (2007) *School leadership and student outcomes: identifying what works and why*, Winmalee, Australian Council for Educational Leaders (Monograph 41, ACEL Monograph Series).

Short KH (2016) 'Intentional, explicit, systematic: implementation and scale-up of effective practices for supporting student well-being in Ontario schools', *International Journal of Mental Health Promotion*, 18(1):33–48.

Victorian Auditor-General (2010) *The effectiveness of student wellbeing programs and services*, Victorian Government Printer, Melbourne.

Watkins C (2004) 'Reclaiming pastoral care', *Pastoral Care in Education*, 22(2):3–6.

Watkins C (1999) 'The case for restructuring the UK secondary school', *Pastoral Care in Education*, 17(4):3–10.

Wylie K (2005) 'The moral dimension of personal and social education', *Pastoral Care in Education*, 23(3):12–8.

Part 1

What's happening?

Assess the school community's wellbeing strengths and needs to determine actions needed to improve staff and student wellbeing

CHAPTER 1

Staff wellbeing is critical for student wellbeing

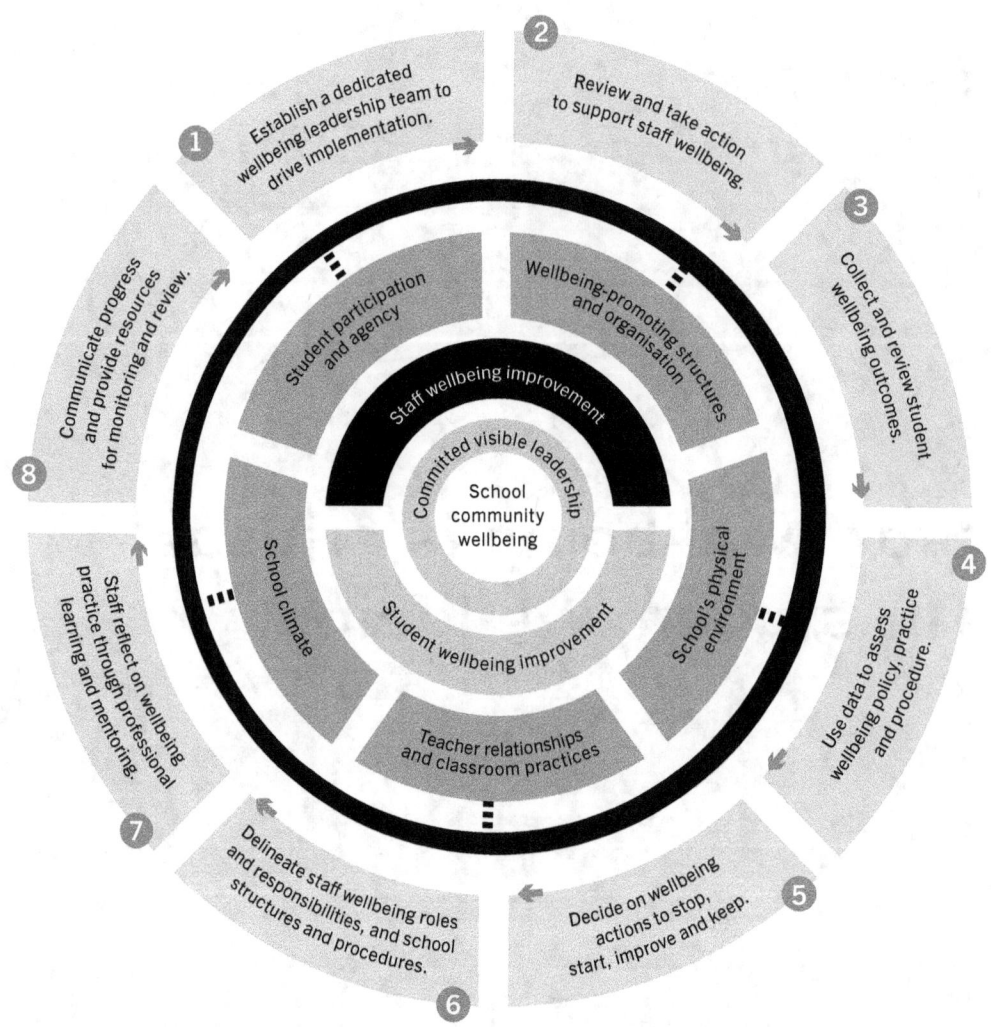

Figure 1.1. Staff wellbeing improvement

School leaders have a responsibility to protect, promote and support their own as well as their staff's wellbeing by creating a healthy school environment. As staff wellbeing is also a critical determinant of student learning, behaviour and wellbeing, school leadership and school staff need to be supported through a framework and strategies that prioritise their own wellbeing. Support and commitment from school leadership is essential in creating a positive school climate in which staff are enabled to review their wellbeing and take action to put policies and practices in place to enhance their own wellbeing. This chapter describes the interrelationship and importance of staff wellbeing to student wellbeing and promoting a healthy whole school community and describes high-impact practices that can be used to develop a staff wellbeing framework.

The importance of staff wellbeing and social environments

Developing young people's academic, social and emotional and behavioural capabilities is highly dependent on skilled, competent and dedicated school staff. Teachers' emotional self-regulation and modelling of social and emotional skills and positive behaviours provides a foundation for positive relationships with their students. However, providing emotional support to students, in addition to the other responsibilities of school staff, can intensify their workload. While teaching is a stressful profession at the best of times, the complexities associated with the COVID-19 pandemic have led to school staff reporting even greater concern for and actions to address the mental health of students, especially for those students who spent long periods of time away from school, learning remotely and being socially isolated (Riley et al. 2021; Thomas et al. 2022).

Prior to the COVID-19 pandemic, school leaders and teachers were already consistently reporting higher levels of work-related stress compared to other occupations. Increased workload, lack of time to focus on teaching or leadership roles, unrealistic workplace expectations and increased levels of stress, anxiety and feeling overwhelmed has put further strain on teachers and school leaders during the pandemic (Burstein 2020; Dabrowski 2020). Staff wellbeing is an important determinant of student learning, behaviour and wellbeing and is needed to effectively support students. Never has it been more important to protect, promote and support staff wellbeing (Cefai and Cavioni 2013; Be You 2021).

Relationship between staff wellbeing and social environments

Student wellbeing is significantly associated with teacher wellbeing largely through the quality of the teacher–student relationship. Exhausted and overwhelmed teachers, for example, are less likely to forge positive relationships with students (see Chapter 4 for more about this).

An individual's overall wellbeing is dependent on their social, mental, emotional, physical and spiritual health. The ecological theory of human development (Bronfenbrenner 1995) illustrates the importance of relationships within and across communities and wider societies. It provides a useful framework to describe the relationship between school staff wellbeing and how this can be influenced by the environment (see Figure 1.2). School staff wellbeing is influenced directly and indirectly by their immediate and wider social environments including family, peers, workplace, community and government.

Individual factors that impact on school staff wellbeing include their personal attitudes, perceived capabilities, perceptions, communication, social and emotional skills, resiliency and self-efficacy (McCallum et al. 2017; Price and McCallum 2015; Biggio and Cortese 2013). Relationships with peers and family have the greatest influence on an individual and are also critical for wellbeing (Herselman et al. 2018; Deci et al. 1991). As shown in Figure 1.2, both the number of relationships and the quality of these interactions with family, friends and peers build a sense of belonging and connectedness, contributing to personal social capital and increased wellbeing (Helliwell and Putnam 2004). School values and school climate (see Chapter 3), relationships with other school staff (see Chapter 4), organisational functioning (see Chapter 6) and the physical or built school environment (see Chapter 7) also significantly impact staff wellbeing, as does the school system and government policies (Biggio and Cortese 2013).

Staff wellbeing is critical for student wellbeing

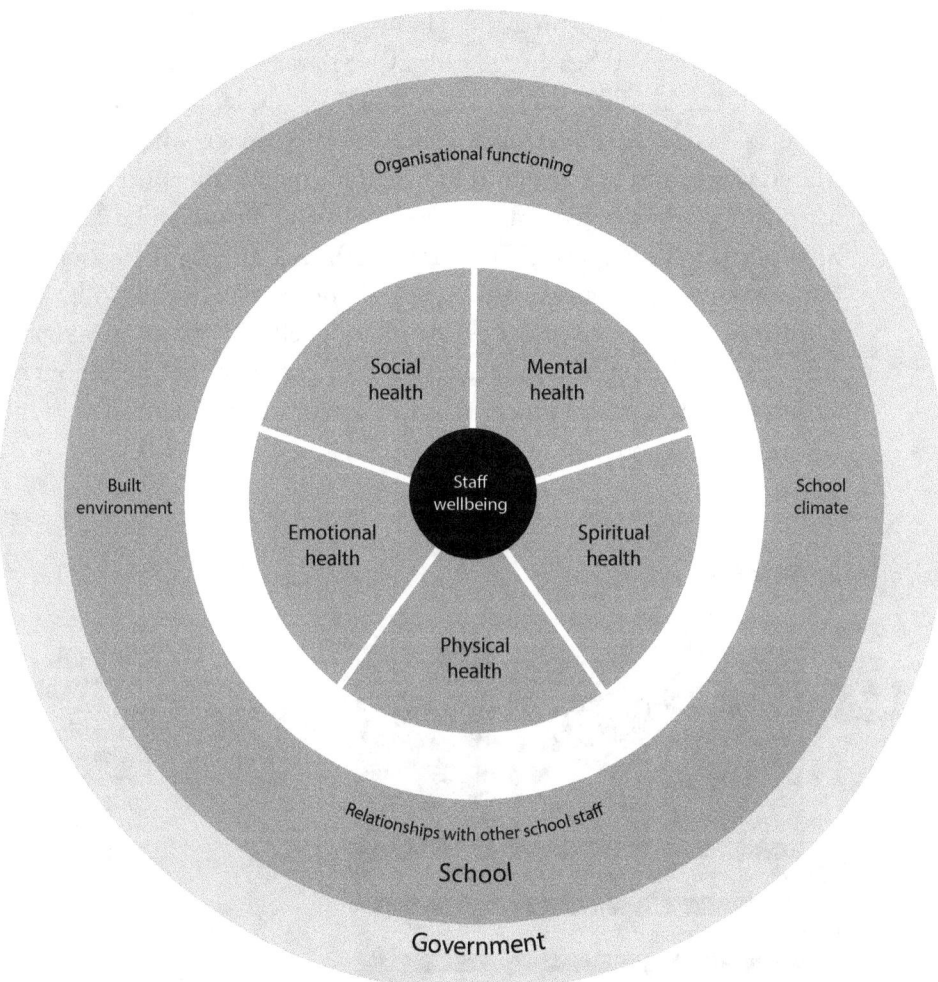

Figure 1.2. Relationship between staff wellbeing and social environments

School leader and staff wellbeing

School leaders have a critical influence on the whole school's wellbeing; their leadership, decisions, strengths, capabilities and their wellbeing significantly influence the education, health and social wellbeing outcomes of students and the professional and wellbeing outcomes of school staff (Robinson 2008; Hallinger and Heck 1996; Robinson 2011; Leithwod and Seashore-Louis 2011; Bayar 2016). A meta-analysis by Scallon et al. (2021) found that practices implemented by school leaders, such as empowering and motivating teachers and building a shared vision and values, matter more than their leadership style (e.g. instructional, distributed, transformational). The Australian Professional Standard for Principals (AITSL 2014: 10) lists among its leadership requirements, 'personal qualities, social and interpersonal skills' and within the professional practices, 'developing self and others' (see Figure 1.3). The wellbeing of principals is thereby critical to the wellbeing of all school staff, which in turn is an important determinant of student learning, behaviour and wellbeing (Cefai and Cavioni 2013).

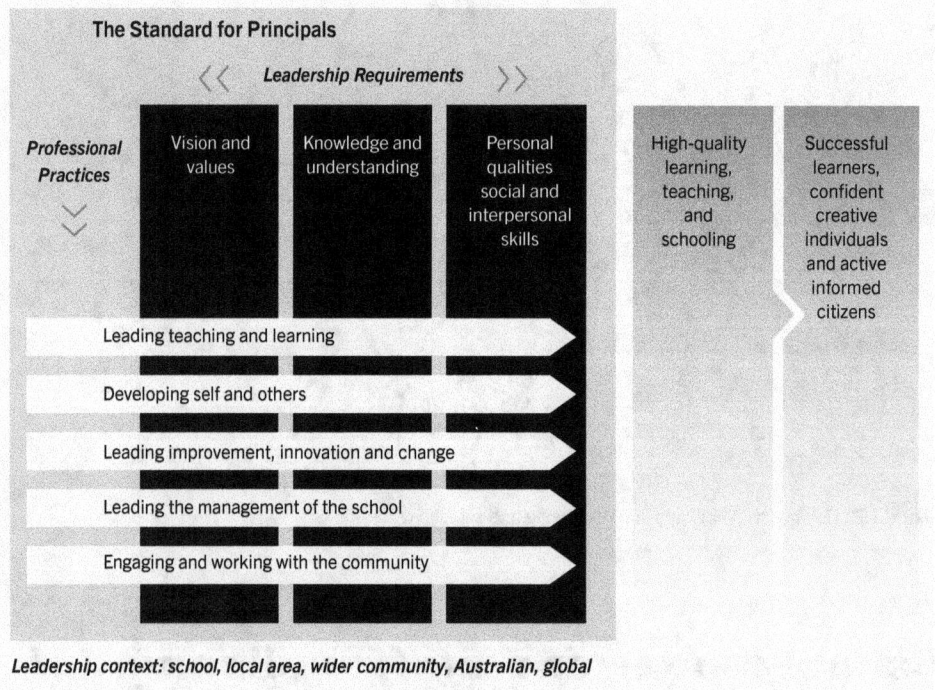

© 2022 Australian Institute for Teaching and School Leadership Limited

Figure 1.3. Leadership context: school, local area, wider community, Australian, global

Source: AITSL (Australian Institute for Teaching and School Leadership) (2014) *Australian professional standard for principals and the leadership profiles*, AITSL, Melbourne. Used with permission.

Principal wellbeing can be adversely affected by many factors (and this was especially apparent during the COVID-19 pandemic), including increasing workload and changing roles; greater emphasis by government on accountability; increasing administrative tasks; the implementation of the national curriculum; public accountability; inadequate support; school size; job demands versus resourcing needs; student- and parent-related issues; exposure to high emotional demands; long work hours; and being subject to offensive behaviour at work (e.g. bullying, harassment, threats, violence, conflicts) (APPA 2017; Riley 2014; Riley 2017). School principals experience higher levels of work-related mental ill-health than people in many other occupations, have poorer levels of exercise and nutrition and elevated risks of cardiovascular disease (APPA 2017; Riley 2014; Riley 2017; Green et al. 2001).

In response to the COVID-19 pandemic, school leaders had to promptly address education disruptions and quickly implement system-level policy directives – leaving many facing extended periods of stress and anxiety (Fotheringham et al. 2021). Leaders were required to manage unprecedented logistics issues related to staff, students and buildings (Beauchamp et al. 2021) while digitising curriculum and implementing new management procedures. The ongoing and unpredictable nature of the role – including these changes caused by the pandemic – is likely impacting principals' mental health and wellbeing (Harris 2020) and their ability to provide effective leadership (Boyland 2011; Reynolds and O'Dwyer 2008).

The most recent longitudinal *Australian principal occupational health, safety and wellbeing survey* (Riley et al. 2021) found school leaders reported worsening results for self-rated long-term health indicators such as stress, burnout, sleeping troubles, depressive symptoms and somatic stress. High principal stress can result in physical ill-health symptoms, low productivity, increased absenteeism, personal relationship difficulties, challenges within the work environment and poor mental health (Sorensen 2007; Murphy 2011). Similarly, the principals surveyed in the Primary Principals' Wellbeing Project reported higher levels of stress, anxiety and depression and lower resilience than population norms, with their job satisfaction and the impact of their work on their home and family life also less favourable than in the general population (CEWA 2016). However, these principals also reported high positive social and emotional wellbeing and had similar physical wellbeing attributes of sleep and exercise to the general population (CEWA 2016). Both positive and negative health behaviours were found to influence principal resilience and wellbeing.

Cross and Falconer (2021) suggest actions to help promote principal and school leader wellbeing include the expansion of staff self-efficacy and coping skills through the provision of effective induction, coaching and mentoring and meaningful professional learning that is sustained and authentic to find and/or sustain work-life balance. This can be achieved through collaborations with retired and current principals and education consultants. Proactive wellbeing strategies such as high-level professional learning programs, professional association connection, access to sabbatical leave, paid access to qualified counselling support, and access to flexible work options and highly skilled administration and executive support, can be employed through all stages of a leadership career.

Teacher and school staff wellbeing is just as important as principal wellbeing. Teachers' wellbeing matters more to student achievement than any other school-related factor (Hattie 2009: Chapter 7). Both nationally and internationally, teachers report high levels of occupational stress, with more than one in 4 Australian teachers reporting emotional exhaustion after starting their careers and expecting to leave teaching within their first 5 years (Milburn 2011). Almost 60% of teachers report not feeling engaged in their work and have considered leaving the profession due to stress (Carroll et al. 2022). A passion for teaching, feeling they are making a difference, and enjoying spending time with students are factors that are highly protective of teacher wellbeing and help the school to function as a caring community. Positive teacher-student relationships have a large, significant effect on students' school connectedness, school adjustment and academic results. These teacher relationship attributes include their warmth, empathy, time spent with students and belief in students' capabilities.

> *In one day we not only teach, we manage behaviour, plan lessons, assess learning, counsel students, carry out first aid, reply to a long list of emails, write reports, tidy classrooms, create resources, mark books and create displays – the list is endless. (The Guardian 28 December 2013)*

Emotionally exhausted teachers may be more likely to use reactive and punitive responses to students that contribute to negative classroom climates and poor student–teacher relationships (Yoon 2002; Osher et al. 2019). Many international and Australian studies (Hascher and Waber 2021; von der Embse et al. 2019) indicate that some teachers report that excessive workload and working hours, adapting and implementing new curriculum, ever-increasing administrative task demands, managing expectations, a lack of acknowledgment and administrative support, assessment, and managing student disruptive behaviour, motivation and attitudes can add to the stress faced in the workplace. Poor communication between staff and leadership and conflict with leadership and colleagues can also lead to highly stressful working conditions. Twenty-three per cent of teachers surveyed in NSW through the People Matter NSW Public Sector Employee Survey 2022 reported they had witnessed bullying in the workplace and 14% had experienced bullying. Bullying of some teachers has taken the form of unmanageable workloads, being ignored or excluded from decision-making, having their integrity undermined, losing or gaining responsibilities without consultation, having personal property attacked, and physical abuse and threats of violence (Riley et al. 2011; Davis and Davis 2007).

Barriers to school leader and teacher wellbeing can be categorised into the following 4 areas: workplace, work conditions, school climate and expectations (Figure 1.4).

BARRIERS TO SCHOOL STAFF WELLBEING

Workload	Workplace conditions	School climate	Expectations
School leaders • Increasing and changing roles • Increased administrative tasks • Introduction of a national curriculum • Demands versus resourcing **Teachers** • Student welfare • Deadlines • Excessive workload and working hours • Adapting and implementing new curriculum	**School leaders** • Inadequate support • School size • Long work hours • Offensive behaviour, such as bullying **Teachers** • Poor student behaviour, motivation, attitude, work ethic • Inadequate resources • Pressure from administration • Lack of administrative support • Geographical isolation	**School leaders** • Student and parent issues • Exposure to high emotional demands **Teachers** • Low positive acknowledgement • Management of bullying/aggression/abuse/threats of violence from parents, students and colleagues • Conflict with administration and colleagues • Limited professional opportunities • Lack of involvement in decision-making • New practices not widely accepted by peers • Integrity undermined • Losing/gaining responsibility without consultation • Poor communication between staff and leadership	**School leaders** • Emphasis on accountability • Public accountability • Parent expectations **Teachers** • Assessment targets • Immediate responses to requests • Efficacy and learning new skills • Parent expectations

Figure 1.4. Barriers to school staff wellbeing

Enabling principal and staff wellbeing

Job satisfaction is related to student achievement for both principals and teachers, with both reporting higher job satisfaction than other professions in The OECD Teaching and Learning International Survey (Dicke et al. 2020, OECD 2020). Supportive relationships and satisfaction with life can enhance physical and mental health, as can the desire to make a difference through being a passionate educator (Lubben et al. 2006). Similarly, individuals who use their strengths and have the ability to develop and adapt are less likely to experience stress, are more resilient and are more likely to achieve their goals (Miglianico et al, 2020). Adaptive or constructive coping, such as seeking social support and reasoned and deliberate problem-solving when experiencing difficulties, reduces psychological distress and improves wellbeing (Chesney et al. 2006). Sleep and physical activity both contribute positively to an individual's resilience (Lee et al. 2015; Ströhle 2009), whereas work–life imbalance, work disengagement and job dissatisfaction often contribute to high levels of stress, detract from a person's quality of life and are detrimental to their wellbeing (Greenhaus et al. 2003; Kofodimos 1993; Bellavia and Frone 2005; Schaufeli and Bakker 2004; Macdonald and MacIntyre 1997).

The importance of providing and promoting a heathy workplace for all school staff is paramount, given the outcomes of an unhealthy workplace. Work-related poor mental health has become a major issue due to the personal cost to the employee, with workplace stress-related claims increasing, resulting in high costs to the employer in terms of productivity (WorkCover Western Australia 2021).

Figure 1.5 illustrates the impact of an unhealthy school versus a healthy school on workplace-related stress, personal health, social outcomes, workplace productivity and student wellbeing. Work-related stress impacts staff, their families and the whole school community. Whereas, an embedded positive school climate characterised by the whole community feeling a strong sense of belonging and common goals, caring and collegial relationships and meaningful and influential engagement, contributes to increased community wellbeing and resilience (Lester et al. 2020). The collaboration of leadership and staff to continually improve the health and safety of all staff results in a healthy workplace.

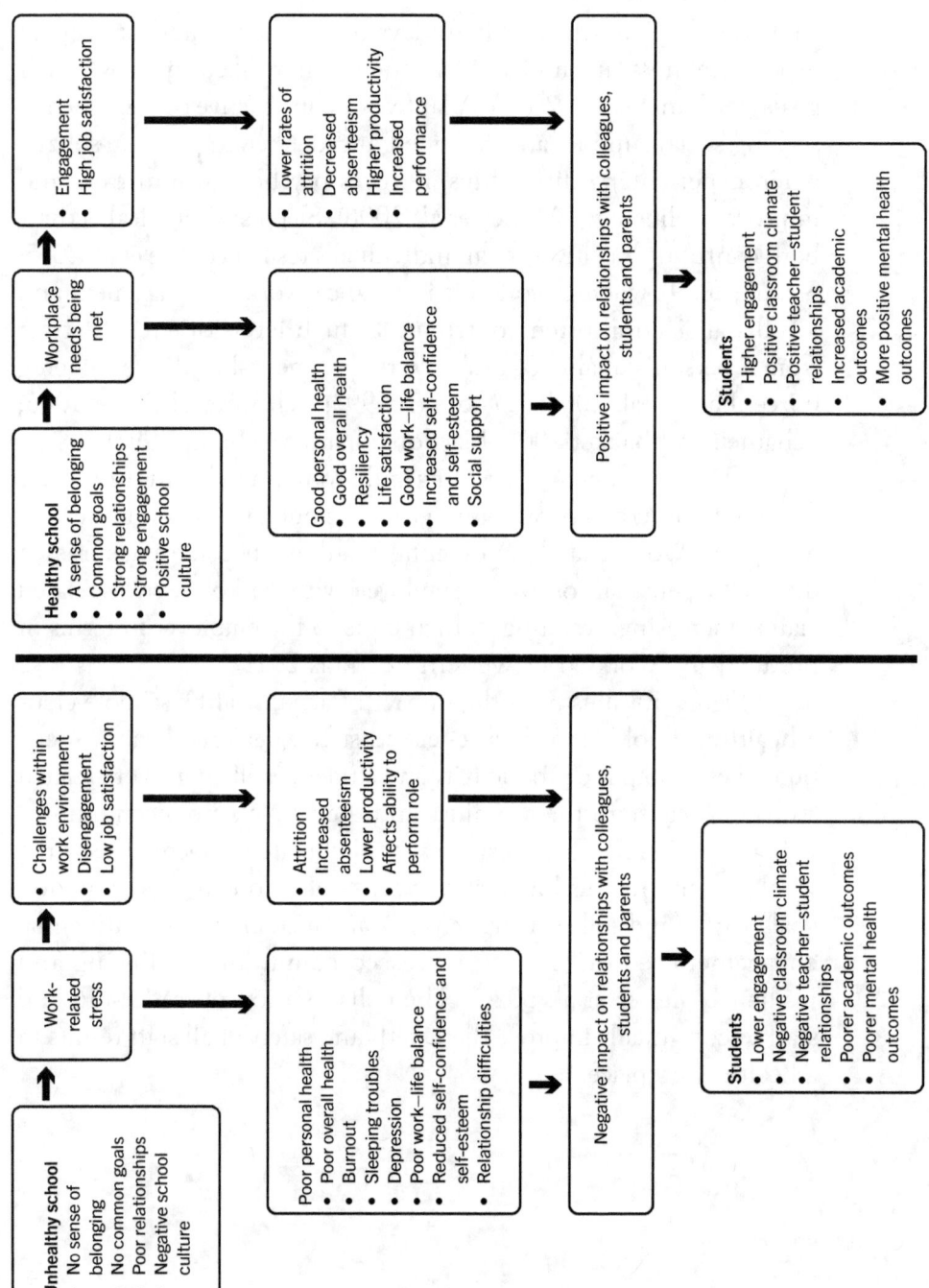

Figure 1.5. Outcomes of an unhealthy versus a healthy school

Enabling staff wellbeing in the COVID-19 era

Being aware of the additional burden faced by school leaders and teachers during the pandemic and other major challenges such as floods and fires, helps to future-proof planning strategies for school community wellbeing. Prioritising equitable and appropriate allocation of resources and professional development focusing on social and emotional learning for school leaders, teachers and students is critical (Harris and Jones 2020; Hamilton et al. 2020).

To mitigate the impact of a pandemic or other major challenge on school leaders, burnout can be reduced by:

> managing and addressing work overload, ensuring social support (Stephenson and Bauer 2010) between peers, colleagues and the wider school community (Beausaert et al. 2016)

> investing in communication systems that encourage cooperation (Fotheringham et al. 2021)

> allocating time to practise self-care (Harris and Jones 2020) and recognising the importance of work–life balance

> enacting distributed leadership (Harris 2020) and crisis management training (Reid 2022) to enhance current and future school leaders' capacity to support themselves and the school community.

Supporting teachers in the wake of a pandemic or other major challenges requires the implementation of organisational-level wellbeing initiatives to reduce fatigue, increase motivation and improve social and emotional wellbeing. 'Teaching is successful when connection is strong' (Flack et al. 2020: 4), therefore building collective efficacy and social capital by focusing on relationships to enhance community bonds is essential (Dabrowski 2020).

Further, Collie (2021) emphasises the strong links between autonomy-supportive leadership and greater resilience and reduced stress and emotional exhaustion in teachers, highlighting the importance of quality leadership and guidance especially during disruptive times. Ensuring there are school-wide initiatives to support teachers, such as including integration of teacher voice in policy and practice (Heffernen et al. 2019: 14), enabling collaboration and connection among the school community, providing timely, applicable and effective professional learning (particularly stress management), resilience (Baker et al. 2021) and regular staff recognition are also critical practice inclusions.

Teacher resilience can protect against the negative impacts of stressors (Howard and Johnson 2004) and correlates with self-efficacy, professional development, commitment and mentorship (Beltman et al. 2011; Patterson et al. 2005). There is also a need for system-level reforms to strengthen teacher professional development in order to cope with long-term disruptions, such as just-in-time technical support for teachers and brief, flexible and blended professional development (Beteille et al. 2020).

Staff wellbeing frameworks

The school is an important health-promoting context that can positively impact staff wellbeing if it is operating as a caring community (Lester et al. 2020). School staff wellbeing frameworks target the whole school and link wellbeing to the individual staff member's engagement and commitment to enhancing their own wellbeing, the wellbeing culture within the school, the culture of wellbeing built by the school system through its strategic direction and systematic approaches (Allison et al 2021; Teach in the Territory 2018; Be You 2021; Garland et al. 2018) and even staff key performance indicators. Wellbeing frameworks aim to improve the school staff's physical health; financial health such as financial literacy and budgeting; occupational wellbeing; psychological wellbeing, including mental health, resilience and stress management; and social and community engagement (DET 2018).

Most of these school staff wellbeing frameworks encourage a step-by-step process, with many including the following common elements:

1. Demonstrate leadership support and commitment.
2. Engage staff in a review of their own wellbeing.

3. Identify and assess staff needs and actions already taken by the school to support staff wellbeing.
4. Develop an action plan.
5. Monitor, evaluate and conduct a regular review of the action plan.

Leadership demonstrate support for staff wellbeing when they demonstrate it is a priority, engage staff in decision-making to improve their wellbeing in the workplace, assess and monitor wellbeing and establish a school staff wellbeing team. There are many strategies at the individual, relationship and school level that can be used to support staff wellbeing, ranging from health promotion, prevention of problems and protective actions, to those addressing early intervention and support (see Figure 1.6). It is important for schools to invest across the wellbeing continuum, as the benefits from the investment in prevention and treatment for both the staff member and the school outweigh the costs (see Figure 1.5).

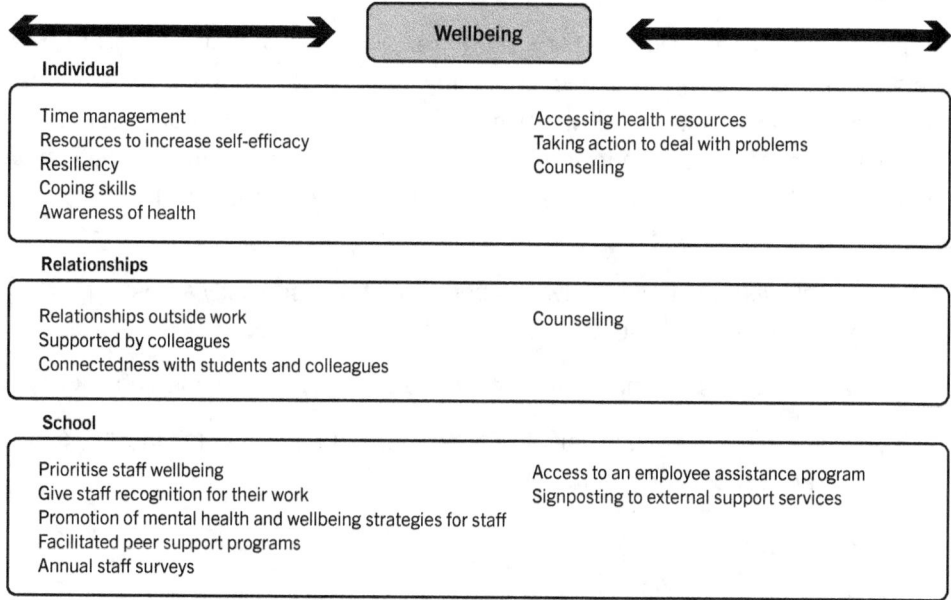

Figure 1.6. Strategies to promote staff wellbeing

Demonstrate leadership support and commitment

Support and commitment from leadership for staff wellbeing, embedded in the school climate, is essential to increase the sustainability and effectiveness of staff wellbeing programs. The school climate (discussed in detail in Chapter 3) needs to provide staff with support and recognition, ensure staff are listened to and appreciated, and encourage and enable positive relationships among colleagues (Garland et al. 2018). In schools with high levels of staff wellbeing, wellbeing is typically prioritised, with internal support from colleagues and mentors and access to employee assistance programs (EAP) and other external supports provided. These schools also promote and protect mental health and implement other wellbeing strategies for staff. They provide stress management programs, positive psychology interventions and targeted specialist support to help staff manage themselves socially and emotionally, and also enable staff to have the capacity to support students (Flook et al. 2010; Woodward 2006).

Leadership practice idea: case study

As part of a school-wide strategic imperative, this school supported the implementation of a whole-school wellbeing framework to provide substantial professional development, staff wellbeing initiatives and in-depth data collection and analysis to monitor, enhance and support overall staff wellbeing. The wellbeing team received feedback that these actions could not be frivolous. The following actions were embedded in the staff wellbeing program:

- social events to build fellowship between staff, especially across departments and sub-schools
- wellbeing classes and onsite preventive and protective health checks
- care and support, e.g. staff who are new parents, promotion of EAP, peer-to-peer support program
- service, e.g. 'casual for a cause'
- recognition, e.g. 'staff appreciation lunch'
- special events, e.g. department picnic baskets, staff retreats
- hypercare for staff experiencing serious personal or health difficulties.

Engage staff in a review of their own wellbeing

Staff wellbeing is a shared responsibility and involves encouraging all staff to make a commitment to their wellbeing as individuals and to creating a supportive school environment and culture. The leadership team can work to improve the wellbeing of all staff by investigating how the ethos or culture of the school impacts on staff wellbeing, reviewing work-related stressors in terms of structures, strategies and processes and the use of a shared language around wellbeing. A staff wellbeing team is necessary to oversee the planning, intervention activities, resource requirements and monitoring and evaluation of staff wellbeing. Regular meetings by the staff wellbeing team can ensure structures and processes are implemented to help minimise work-related stressors and regular staff fellowship events are organised to help staff practise ways to protect and promote their own wellbeing.

The creation of a staff wellbeing team is detailed in the section 'Develop an action plan'. A graffiti wall in the staff room, for example, could showcase one issue at a time for a week to encourage staff involvement and recommendations (e.g. large sheets of butcher's paper set up in the staff room for staff to record considerations and/or recommended actions in accordance with the question/statement written on the sheets). As different issues may affect various groups of staff in different ways, sub-groups could be formed and aligned within the school organisational chart (e.g. teachers work with other teachers, heads of house work with other heads of house) to suggest specific actions they can take in their roles to improve their own wellbeing.

Professional development opportunities are an important starting point to build staff capacity and self-efficacy to reduce and manage stress and to improve their mental wellbeing, resilience and coping skills. Organisations like Be You (2023) and WISA (n.d.) aim to improve wellbeing within schools and offer training, mentorship and support. Staff should also be encouraged and supported via professional/personal development to review what actions they can take to enhance their own and their colleagues' physical, emotional, mental and social wellbeing.

Identify and assess staff needs and actions already taken by the school to support staff wellbeing

The health and wellbeing of school staff needs to be monitored and addressed. It is important to involve all school staff to identify both their individual and collective wellbeing needs and to benchmark (and then monitor) overall staff wellbeing before they co-develop and implement practices. This needs assessment can be led by the team responsible for supporting staff wellbeing.

Both qualitative (interviews and discussion groups) and quantitative (survey) methods should be used to measure and understand the effectiveness of the school structures, processes, policies and procedures in place to support staff wellbeing and to identify areas for improvement. The staff wellbeing team can use these staff wellbeing data to develop recommendations and implement actions (such as those described in Table 1.1 on p. 35) to improve staff wellbeing.

Each school-level structure, process, policy and procedure can be reviewed to determine the impact it has on wellbeing. This can involve considering elements worthy of maintaining, those needing improvement, those that should be stopped and others that are missing. This review process is illustrated in Figure 1.7.

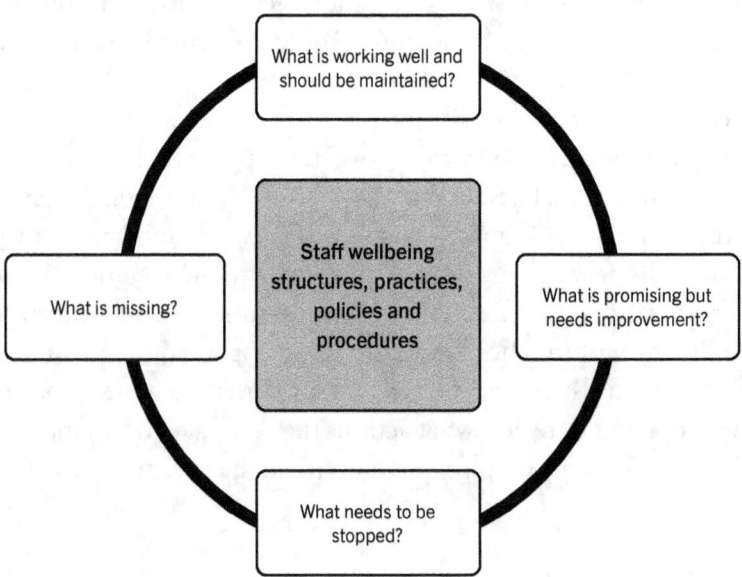

Figure 1.7. Reviewing school structures, processes, policies and procedures that impact staff wellbeing

Leadership practice idea: case study

To engage staff in the promotion of wellbeing for themselves and their students, staff were provided with professional development in Youth Mental Health First Aid training, the Gatekeeper Suicide Prevention course and mindfulness training. This school also focused on staff wellbeing, using surveys and interviews to gather suggestions about how to better support them to do their jobs. Efforts were also made to reduce the administration expectations of staff, so they could better focus on core tasks and use more of their energy to benefit the students.

Understanding staff wellbeing at the school level

In a study of Australian schools, less than one-quarter of teachers surveyed reported that their schools regularly survey their staff to understand their overall wellbeing (Lester et al. 2020). A survey tool to identify personal strengths and needs of school staff and whole-school impacts on their wellbeing can help to identify targets of intervention and outline a plan of action. Annual or biannual staff wellbeing surveys, where overall results are presented to staff for reflection, discussion and planning, create ownership, allow staff to be engaged in identifying actions to improve their own wellbeing and ensure staff wellbeing initiatives meet their needs.

The impact of school structures, policies, practices and procedures on staff wellbeing can be collected using a survey at the whole-school level that measures the following indicators (Cefai and Cavioni 2013):

> caring and supportive relationships with leadership, colleagues and the student and parent community

> staff feeling actively engaged

> support for staff emotional wellbeing.

A checklist at the end of this chapter contains sample survey questions that can be used to review high-impact practices needed to improve wellbeing.

Supportive relationships within the school community

The following supportive relationships indicators can be used to measure and identify areas of staff need. Staff should feel:

- ❯ valued, respected and supported by the school leadership team
- ❯ that their wellbeing is considered important by the school leadership team
- ❯ valued, respected and supported by their colleagues
- ❯ that they have opportunities to come together to support each other and consider ways to address problems together
- ❯ that they have appropriately transparent communication within the school community.

The survey to assess these indicators could also include items measuring caring and supportive relationships between colleagues, with the school administration and leadership, and relationships with the broader school community, such as students and parents/carers.

Leadership practice idea: case study

A factor affecting school staff morale and wellbeing in this school was the perceived equity of resources to support staff across the school. For example, the senior school staffroom had a coffee machine and staff were provided with fruit for morning tea, whereas no coffee machine or fruit was provided in the junior school staffroom (which was also a fair walk from the senior staffroom). The leadership team arranged to provide the junior school staff with better coffee and fruit to show they were equally valued. The leadership team recognised other more significant changes were also needed to support staff wellbeing, which would require more time to implement, but their quick action on easier tasks was a demonstration to staff that they were listening.

Staff feeling actively engaged

The leadership team can also put procedures in place to support and promote staff collaboration and constructive conflict resolution, and encourage collegiality through enabling partnerships such as communities of practice, mentoring and the sharing of resources (Lester et al. 2020:32). To assess staff engagement, the following indicators could be used:

> - Staff are actively encouraged to be involved in school activities.
> - Staff are actively encouraged to contribute to staff meetings.
> - Staff are actively encouraged to collaborate by sharing practices and resources.
> - Staff partnerships, mentorships and support networks are available and encouraged.
> - Staff are consulted to determine what wellbeing support they need.
> - Staff are provided with adequate support, resources and technology for their work.

Support for staff emotional wellbeing

Emotional wellbeing indicators include measures of a school's provision of support for staff social and emotional needs, positive emotional wellbeing and development. By regularly recognising and acknowledging staff and their contributions and assessing and positively modifying supporting structures, the leadership team can positively impact staff wellbeing.

> *Developing the positive wellbeing of staff has made a huge difference. When teaching staff feel appreciated and empowered, they are much more likely to show patience and empathy for their students; to go the 'extra mile' for the students in their care. They*

are also more likely to share and work with others to support their students and promote wellbeing. (Roffey 2012: 8)

This can also be enhanced by identifying and offering learning opportunities and professional development for staff (Margolis 2006), providing mentors and coaching for interested staff (Squires 2019) and by clearly communicating policies and practices that address staff bullying, harassment or discrimination (Konu 2010). The following indicators can be used to identify and measure areas in which the school leadership team can support staff emotional wellbeing:

- Staff emotional wellbeing is a school priority.
- Staff emotional wellbeing is being measured and monitored.
- Professional learning to support staff wellbeing is offered to all staff.
- Internal and/or external mentors are available for interested staff.
- Staff coaching is provided in work management skills.
- Support structures for staff are clearly communicated.
- External support services are provided for all staff.
- Designated areas are provided to enable all staff to take a break.
- Designated quiet work areas are available for staff.
- Staff are given opportunities to connect socially with each other.

Individual indicators of wellbeing

Surveys are best used to measure domains of staff wellbeing (such as workplace, social and emotional, mental and physical wellbeing) and the success of wellbeing programs, initiatives and services. Reliable and validated scales are freely available (e.g. SDQ, a strengths and difficulties measure [Goodman 1997]; DASS, measuring depression, anxiety and stress [Lovibond and Lovibond 1995]; and the Brief Resilience Scale for resiliency [Smith et al. 2008]) and can be used to measure staff wellbeing, with results compared to normative data. Examples of staff wellbeing indicators that could be measured via a survey are listed in Table 1.1.

Table 1.1. Staff wellbeing indicator

WELLBEING DOMAINS	WELLBEING INDICATORS			
Workplace	Work–life balance	Work engagement	Job satisfaction	Work stress
Social and emotional	Social networks	Personal growth	Use of strengths	Happiness
Mental	Resilience	Mindfulness	Coping strategies	Depression
Physical	Physical activity	Sleep duration	Sleep quality	Healthy diet

Develop an action plan

Using the staff wellbeing data, the school wellbeing team can develop a tailored action plan to promote staff wellbeing that outlines wellbeing goals and procedures and implements and evaluates wellbeing strategies. Effective staff wellbeing initiatives typically comprise multiple strategies implemented over time.

A staff wellbeing action plan will include clear goals and objectives co-developed with staff members. Goals and objectives will be based on current staff wellbeing (as measured in the needs assessment) and what staff wellbeing may look like in the future.

The creation of a staff wellbeing team will increase a sense of ownership and engagement by staff members. Ideally, this team will involve representatives from the leadership team, teaching and non-teaching staff members and staff from each sub-school. The team typically takes responsibility for the implementation of the staff wellbeing program and for setting wellbeing targets, allocating tasks to team members and other interested staff. For each wellbeing strategy, specific activities need to be defined, with resources required, a timeline and how success will be measured.

An evaluation of the wellbeing plan and individual wellbeing activities and strategies needs to be built into the action plan. The timing and extent of the evaluation also needs to be detailed to monitor processes, progress and outcomes. An example of an action plan is presented in Table 1.2.

Table 1.2. Action plan to promote staff wellbeing

GOAL: PROMOTE POSITIVE MENTAL HEALTH AND WELLBEING OBJECTIVE: TO REDUCE STAFF WORK-RELATED STRESS OVER 12 MONTHS					
Strategies	Activities	Time frame	People responsible	Resources required	Measuring success
Celebrate staff achievements	Morning tea	Weekly	Leadership team	Leadership time Venue Budget for food and drink A roster for food	Number of staff participating in morning tea
Encourage staff to work together on specific wellbeing tasks	One-day staff workshops	Once a term	Head of department	Head of department and staff time Venue	Post-strategy survey
Encourage mindfulness	Mindfulness program or engage an external provider	February–November	Wellbeing team, train the trainer model	Budget for program or external provider Wellbeing team member time	Pre- and post-survey on mindfulness
Encourage staff to take part in social activities	Staff lead and organise activities, dates and times Promote activities	Term 2 and Term 3	Wellbeing team	Wellbeing team time	Number of staff participating in social events
Encourage staff to access employee assistance programs	Staff email	Once a term	Wellbeing team	Wellbeing team time	Increased awareness of availability of services

Monitor, evaluate and conduct a regular review of the action plan

Whole-school approaches to enhance staff wellbeing need to be continually monitored with regular evaluation to measure school improvement in staff wellbeing. Monitoring, evaluation and review of the staff wellbeing strategy and action plan helps to ensure it is contributing to a positive school culture and enhancing staff wellbeing. Monitoring, evaluation and review enables the school to:

> measure the success of each strategy
> measure the success of the overall program
> assess the outcome of time, effort and resources
> know what worked for whom, when and under what circumstances
> determine what needs to be modified moving forward
> disseminate results showing leadership action on issues identified.

Reviewing staff wellbeing is an ongoing process. Annual staff surveys provide insight into the impact of actions taken to improve wellbeing and enable a review of the effectiveness of wellbeing strategies and the wellbeing program overall, compared to the baseline needs assessment results. Successes need to be celebrated and communicated to all staff. Key dates for the evaluation or review of the action plan need to be detailed and reviewed at least every school semester.

To develop a school staff wellbeing framework, support and commitment from leadership is essential in engaging staff, assessing needs, developing an action plan, and in monitoring and evaluating the action plan. The questions in Table 1.3 will assist in starting to develop a staff wellbeing framework.

Table 1.3. Questions to assist with developing a staff wellbeing framework

Why	Why is a staff wellbeing plan needed and what are the overarching goals?
	What are our specific objectives and strategies and why are they needed?
Who	Who will head up the staff wellbeing team?
	Who is responsible for planning the staff wellbeing strategy and activities?
	Who is responsible for setting targets?
How	How will the team be formed?
	How will the staff wellbeing activities be funded?
	How will all staff members be given the opportunity to be involved in the staff wellbeing planning and activities?
	How will staff monitor their progress in the staff wellbeing activities?
	How will the effectiveness of these activities be monitored?
What	In what order do the staff wellbeing activities need to be delivered?
	What implementation tasks need to be considered and by whom?
	What are potential barriers to staff engaging in the wellbeing initiatives and how can they be overcome?
When	When will the staff wellbeing activities be delivered?
	For how long are each of the staff wellbeing activities planned to be implemented?
	When will the staff wellbeing activities be evaluated and by whom?
Where	Where will the staff wellbeing activities occur?

Chapter summary

This chapter outlines in detail the 5-step process that can be used to guide schools' development of a school staff wellbeing improvement plan and actions to support staff wellbeing, led by a school wellbeing team. Principal and staff wellbeing directly impacts student wellbeing and is influenced by many factors within the school environment including workload, work conditions, school climate and expectations. A staff wellbeing framework aims to improve school staff's overall health, through encouraging self-determination and a positive school culture. The following checklist can be used to review high-impact practices needed to improve staff wellbeing.

In our school, staff feel that:	Not in place	Working towards	In place	Progressing well
Their wellbeing is being regularly considered by the leadership team, monitored and responded to.				
Actions to improve staff wellbeing have been co-developed in consultation with staff.				
A staff wellbeing team has been appointed.				
A wellbeing policy is in place that addresses the needs of staff.				
Meetings are held regularly to address staff wellbeing.				
There is a whole-school culture of staff help seeking and help support.				
There is a system of mentors from whom staff can seek advice and support.				
Workloads are regularly reviewed to encourage work–life balance.				
They have access to external sources of support.				
Opportunities are provided for them to come together to support each other and work through problems together.				
A dedicated comfortable physical space is provided for them to take time out.				
They have opportunities to provide positive feedback to each other.				
They receive appropriate recognition for their work.				
They receive the resources they need to teach effectively.				
They are provided with professional development to support their own wellbeing.				
Positive whole-staff social activities are encouraged to build fellowship and are free or low-cost.				
Positive social interactions between staff and students are encouraged.				
Regular staff wellbeing surveys are implemented and findings monitored.				

References

Achenbach TM (2015) *Developmental psychopathology*, Oxford University Press, Oxford.

AITSL (Australian Institute for Teaching and School Leadership) (2014) *Australian professional standard for principals and the leadership profiles*, AITSL, Melbourne, accessed 18 January 2023. https://www.aitsl.edu.au/docs/default-source/national-policy-framework/australian-professional-standard-for-principals-and-the-leadership-profiles.pdf?sfvrsn=c07eff3c_24

Allison, L., Perich, D. & Steven, S. (2021). CEWA Strategic Wellbeing Framework. Catholic Education Western Australia, Perth.

APPA (Australian Primary Principals Association) (2017) *Back to balance: how policy and practice can make primary principals highly effective*, APPA, Stirling, ACT.

Askell-Williams H, Lawson MJ, Skrzypiec G (2012) 'Scaffolding cognitive and metacognitive strategy instruction in regular class lessons', *Instructional Science*, 40(2):413–443.

Baker CN, Peele H, Daniels M, Saybe M, Whalen K, Overstreet S, Trauma-Informed Schools Learning Collaborative The New Orleans (2021) 'The experience of COVID-19 and its impact on teachers' mental health, coping, and teaching', *School Psychology Review*, 50(4):491–504.

Bayar A (2016) 'Challenges facing principals in the first year at their schools', Universal *Journal of Educational Research*, 4(1):192–199.

Beauchamp G, Hulme M, Clarke L, Hamilton L, Harvey JA (2021) '"People miss people": a study of school leadership and management in the four nations of the United Kingdom in the early stage of the COVID-19 pandemic', *Educational Management Administration & Leadership*, 49(3):375–392.

Beausaert S, Froehlich DE, Devos C, Riley P (2016) 'Effects of support on stress and burnout in school principals', *Educational Research*, 58:347–365.

Bellavia GM, Frone MR (2005) 'Work-family conflict', in Barling J, Kelloway EK, Frone M (eds) *Handbook of work stress*, Sage Publications, Thousand Oaks, California.

Beltman S, Mansfield C, Price A (2011) 'Thriving not just surviving: a review of research on teacher resilience', *Educational Research Review*, 6(3):185–207.

Beteille T, Ding E, Molina E, Pushparatnam A, Wilichowski T (2020) *Three principles to support teacher effectiveness during COVID-19*, World Bank, Washington, DC.

Be You (2021) *Staff wellbeing*, BeYou website, accessed 19 January 2023. https://beyou.edu.au/fact-sheets/your-wellbeing/staff-wellbeing

Be You (2023) *BeYou* [website], accessed 26 January 2023. https://beyou.edu.au/

Biggio G, Cortese C (2013) 'Well-being in the workplace through interaction between individual characteristics and organizational context', *International Journal of Qualitative Studies on Health and Well-being*, 8(1):19823.

Boyland LG (2011) 'Job stress and coping strategies of elementary principals: a statewide study', *Current Issues in Education*, 14(3).

Bronfenbrenner U (1995) 'Developmental ecology through space and time: a future perspective', in Moen P, Elder GH, Luscher K (eds) *Examining lives in context: perspectives on the ecology of human development*, American Psychological Association, Washington, DC.

Burstein R (2020) *Research eclipsed: how educators are reinventing research-informed practice during the pandemic*, EdSurge Research, Portland, OR.

Carroll A, Forrest K, Sanders-O'Connor E, Flynn L, Bower JM, Fynes-Clinton S, York A, Ziaei M (2022) 'Teacher stress and burnout in Australia: examining the role of intrapersonal and environmental factors' *Soc Psychol Educ,* 22(2–3):441–469, doi:10.1007/s11218-022-09686-7.

Cefai C, Cavioni V (2013) *Social and emotional education in primary school: integrating theory and research into practice*, Springer, New York.

CEWA (Catholic Education WA) (2016) *Primary Principals' Wellbeing Project*, Catholic Education Western Australia.

Chesney MA, Neilands TB, Chambers DB, Taylor JM, Folkman S (2006) 'A validity and reliability study of the coping self-efficacy scale', *British Journal of Health Psychology*, 11(3):421–437.

Clandinin DJ, Long J, Schaefer L, Downey CA, Steeves P, Pinnegar E, McKenzie Robblee S, Wnuk S (2015) 'Early career teacher attrition: intentions of teachers beginning', *Teaching Education*, 26(1):1–16.

Collie RJ (2021) 'COVID-19 and teachers' somatic burden, stress, and emotional exhaustion: examining the role of principal leadership and workplace buoyancy', *AERA Open,* 7.

Coyle-Shapiro JA, Conway N (2005) 'Exchange relationships: examining psychological contracts and perceived organizational support', *Journal of Applied Psychology*, 90(4):774.

Cross D, Falconer S (2021) *School leaders' and staff wellbeing is critical for student success: our schools – our future research paper November 2021*, Independent Schools Queensland, Spring Hill.

Dabrowski A (2020) 'Teacher wellbeing during a pandemic: surviving or thriving?', *Social Education Research*, 2(1):35–40.

Davis S, Davis J (2007) *Schools where everyone belongs: practical strategies for reducing bullying*, Research Press, Champaign, IL.

Deci EL, Vallerand RJ, Pelletier LG, Ryan RM (1991) 'Motivation and education: the self-determination perspective', *Educational Psychologist*, 26(3–4):325–346.

Dicke T, Marsh HW, Parker PD, Guo J, Riley P, Waldeyer J (2020) 'Job satisfaction of teachers and their principals in relation to climate and student achievement', *Journal of Educational Psychology*, 112(5):1061–1073, doi:10.1037/edu0000409.

Education Support Partnership (2018) *Teacher wellbeing index*, Education Support Partnership, London, accessed 19 January 2023. https://www.educationsupport.org.uk/media/drdlozbf/teacher_wellbeing_index_2018.pdf

von der Embse N, Ryan SV, Gibbs T, Mankin A (2019) 'Teacher stress interventions: a systematic review', *Psychology in the Schools*, 56(8):1328–1343.

Falecki D (2015) *Teacher stress and wellbeing literature review*, Unpublished.

Flack CB, Walker L, Bickerstaff A, Earle H, Margetts C (2020) *Educator perspectives on the impact of COVID-19 on teaching and learning in Australia and New Zealand*, Pivot Professional Learning, Melbourne, Australia.

Flook L, Smalley SL, Kitil MJ, Galla BM, Kaiser-Greenland S, Locke J, Ishijima E, Kasari C (2010) 'Effects of mindful awareness practices on executive functions in elementary school children', *Journal of Applied School Psychology*, 26(1):70–95.

Fotheringham P, Harriott T, Healy G, Arenge G, Wilson E (2021) 'Pressures and influences on school leaders navigating policy development during the COVID-19 pandemic', *British Educational Research Journal*, 48(1).

Garland L, Linehan T, Merrett N, Smith J, Payne C (2018) *Ten steps towards school staff wellbeing*, The Anna Freud National Centre for Children and Families, London.

Goodman R (1997) 'The Strengths and Difficulties Questionnaire: a research note', *Journal of Child Psychology and Psychiatry*, 38(5):581–586.

Green R, Malcolm S, Greenwood K, Small M, Murphy G (2001) 'A survey of the health of Victorian primary school principals', *International Journal of Educational Management*, 15(1):23–30.

Greenhaus JH, Collins KM, Shaw JD (2003) 'The relation between work–family balance and quality of life', *Journal of Vocational Behavior*, 63(3):510–531.

Hallinger P, Heck RH (1996) 'Reassessing the principal's role in school effectiveness: a review of empirical research, 1980–1995', *Educational Administration Quarterly*, 32(1):5–44.

Hamilton LS, Kaufman JH, Diliberti MK (2020) *Teaching and leading through a pandemic: key findings from the American Educator Panels spring 2020 COVID-19 surveys*, RAND corporation, Santa Monica, CA.

Harris A (2020) 'COVID-19 – school leadership in crisis?', *Journal of Professional Capital and Community*, 5(3/4):321–326.

Harris A, Jones M (2020) 'COVID-19 – school leadership in disruptive times', *School Leadership & Management*, 40(4):243–247.

Hascher T, Waber J (2021) 'Teacher well-being: a systematic review of the research literature from the year 2000–2019', *Educational Research Review*, 34:100411.

Hattie J (2009) *Visable learning: a synthesis of 800 meta-analyses relating to achievement*, Routledge, New York.

Heffernan A, Longmuir F, Bright D, Kim M (2019) *Perceptions of teachers and teaching in Australia*, Monash University: Faculty of Education.

Helliwell JF, Putnam RD (2004) 'The social context of well–being', *Philosophical Transactions of the Royal Society of London Series B: Biological Sciences*, 359(1449):1435–1446.

Herselman M, Botha A, Mayindi D, Reid E (2018) 'Influences of the ecological systems theory influencing technological use in rural schools in South Africa: a case study', *2018 International Conference on Advances in Big Data, Computing and Data Communication Systems (icABCD)*, 1–8.

Howard S, Johnson B (2004) 'Resilient teachers: resisting stress and burnout', *Social Psychology of Education*, 7(4):399–420.

Kofodimos JR (1993) *Balancing act: how managers can integrate successful careers and fulfilling personal lives*, Jossey-Bass.

Konu A, Viitanen E, Lintonen T (2010) 'Teachers' wellbeing and perceptions of leadership practices', *International Journal of Workplace Health Management*, 3(1):44–57.

Lee SJ, Park CS, Kim BJ, Lee CS, Cha B, Lee D (2015) 'Sleep and resilience', *Sleep Medicine and Psychophysiology*, 22(2):53–56.

Leithwood K, Seashore-Louis K (2011) *Linking leadership to student learning*, John Wiley & Sons, Hoboken, NJ.

Lendrum A, Humphrey N, Wigelsworth M (2013) 'Social and emotional aspects of learning (SEAL) for secondary schools: implementation difficulties and their implications for school-based mental health promotion', *Child and Adolescent Mental Health*, 18(3):158–164.

Lester L, Cefai C, Cavioni V, Barnes A, Cross D (2020) 'A whole-school approach to promoting staff wellbeing', *Australian Journal of Teacher Education*, 45(2):1–22.

Lovibond PF, Lovibond SH (1995) 'The structure of negative emotional states: comparison of the Depression Anxiety Stress Scales (DASS) with the Beck Depression and Anxiety Inventories', *Behaviour Research and Therapy*, 33(3):335–343.

Lubben J, Blozik E, Gillmann G, Iliffe S, von Renteln Kruse W, Beck JC, Stuck AE (2006) 'Performance of an abbreviated version of the Lubben Social Network Scale among three European community-dwelling older adult populations', *The Gerontologist*, 46(4):503–513.

Macdonald S, MacIntyre P (1997) 'The generic job satisfaction scale: scale development and its correlates', *Employee Assistance Quarterly*, 13(2):1–16.

Margolis J, Nagel L (2006) 'Education reform and the role of administrators in mediating teacher stress', *Teacher Education Quarterly*, 33(4):143–159.

McCallum F, Price D, Graham A, Morrison A (2017) *Teacher wellbeing: a review of the literature*, Association of Independent Schools NSW, Sydney, NSW.

Miglianico M, Dubreuil P, Miquelon P, Bakker AB, Martin-Krumm C (2020) 'Strength use in the workplace: a literature review, *Journal of Happiness Studies*, 21(2):737–764.

Milburn C (7 March 2011) 'More teachers but fewer staying the course', *Sydney Morning Herald*, accessed 19 January 2023. https://www.smh.com.au/education/more-teachers-but-fewer-staying-the-course-20110304-1bhuv.html

Murphy JT (2011) 'Dancing in the rain: tips on thriving as a leader in tough times', *Phi Delta Kappan*, 93(1):36–41.

OECD (Organization for Economic Co-operation and Development) (2020) *TALIS 2018 Results (Volume II): teachers and school leaders as valued professionals*, TALIS, OECD Publishing, Paris, doi:10.1787/19cf08df-en.

Osher D, Spier E, Kendziora K, Cai C (2009) 'Improving academic achievement through improving school climate and student connectedness', *Annual Meeting of the American Educational Research Association*, San Diego, CA.

Patterson JH, Collins L, Abbott G (2004) 'A study of teacher resilience in urban schools', *Journal of Instructional Psychology*, 31(1):3–11.

Price D, McCallum F (2015) 'Ecological influences on teachers' well-being and "fitness"', *Asia-Pacific Journal of Teacher Education*, 43(3):195–209.

Reid DB (2022) 'Suppressing and sharing: how school principals manage stress and anxiety during COVID-19', *School Leadership & Management*, 42(1):62–78.

Reinke WM, Stormont M, Herman KC, Puri R, Goel N (2011) 'Supporting children's mental health in schools: teacher perceptions of needs, roles, and barriers', *School Psychology Quarterly*, 26(1):1.

Reynolds CH, O'Dwyer LM (2008) 'Examining the relationships among emotional intelligence, coping mechanisms for stress, and leadership effectiveness for middle school principals', *Journal of School Leadership,* 18(5):472–500.

Riley D, Duncan DJ, Edwards J (2011) 'Staff bullying in Australian schools', *Journal of Educational Administration*, 49(1):7–30.

Riley P (2014) 'Principals' psychological health: it's not just lonely at the top, it's dangerous', Australian Psychological Society, *InPsych 2014*, 36(6).

Riley P (2017) *The Australian principal health and wellbeing survey*, Faculty of Education, Monash University.

Riley P, See S-M, Marsh H, Dicke T (2021) *The Australian principal occupational health, safety and wellbeing survey 2020 data*, Institute for Positive Psychology and Education, Australian Catholic University, Sydney.

Robinson V (2011) *Student-centered leadership*, John Wiley & Sons, New York.

Robinson VM (2008) 'Forging the links between distributed leadership and educational outcomes', *Journal of Educational Administration*, 46(2):241–256.

Roffey S (2012) 'Pupil wellbeing—teacher wellbeing: two sides of the same coin?', *Educational and Child Psychology*, 29(4):8.

Scallon AM, Bristol TJ, Esboldt J (2021) 'Teachers' perceptions of principal leadership practices that influence teacher turnover', *Journal of Research on Leadership Education*, doi:19427751211034214.

Schaufeli WB, Bakker AB (2004) 'Job demands, job resources, and their relationship with burnout and engagement: a multi-sample study', *Journal of Organizational Behavior*, 25(3):293–315.

See S, Kidson P, Marsh H, Dicke T (2015) *The Australian principal occupational health, safety and wellbeing survey*, Institute for Positive Psychology and Education, Australian Catholic University, Sydney.

Simos M (5 April 2011) 'Why our teachers want to leave', *The Advertiser*, accessed 19 January 2023. https://www.adelaidenow.com.au/news/why-our-teachers-want-to-leave/news-story/090e22fe4a138030340ad7705fe057ce

Singhal P (30 October 2018) 'Quarter of high school teachers say they are bullied', *The Sydney Morning Herald*, accessed 19 January 2023. https://www.smh.com.au/education/quarter-of-high-school-teachers-say-they-are-bullied-20181029-p50clt.html

Smith BW, Dalen J, Wiggins K, Tooley E, Christopher P, Bernard J (2008) 'The brief resilience scale: assessing the ability to bounce back', *International Journal of Behavioral Medicine*, 15(3):194–200.

Sorenson RD (2007) 'Stress management in education: warning signs and coping mechanisms', *Management in Education*, 21(3):10–13.

Squires V (2019) 'The well-being of the early career teacher: a review of the literature on the pivotal role of mentoring', *International Journal of Mentoring and Coaching in Education*.

Stephenson LE, Bauer SC (2010) 'The role of isolation in predicting new principals' burnout', *International Journal of Education Policy and Leadership*, 5(9).

Ströhle A (2009) 'Physical activity, exercise, depression and anxiety disorders', *Journal of Neural Transmission*, 116(6):777.

Teach in the Territory (2018) *Educator wellbeing*, Teach in the Territory website, accessed 19 January 2023. https://www.teachintheterritory.nt.gov.au/educator-support/educator-wellbeing

The Guardian (28 December 2013) 'The secret teacher: stress is reaching a crisis point in schools', *The Guardian*, accessed 19 January 2023. https://www.theguardian.com/teacher-network/teacher-blog/2013/dec/28/stress-crisis-teaching-profession-secret-teacher

Thomas HM, Runions KC, Lester L, Lombardi K, Epstein M, Mandzufas J, Barrow T, Ang S, Leahy A, Mullane M, Whelan A, Coffin J, Mitrou F, Zubrick SR, Bowen AC, Gething PW, Cross D (2022) 'Western Australian adolescent emotional wellbeing during the COVID-19 pandemic in 2020', *Child and Adolescent Psychiatry and Mental Health*, 16(1):1–11.

WorkCover Western Australia (2021) *Stress-related workers' compensation claims in WA*, Statistical Note 2021, WorkCover Western Australia, Shenton Park, accessed 27 February 2023. https://www.workcover.wa.gov.au/wp-content/uploads/2021/07/Stress-Related-Workers-Compensation-Claims-Statistical-Note-2021-BISstatrep.pdf

WISA (n.d.) *WISA* [website], accessed 26 January 2023. https://wisawellbeing.com.au

Woodward P (2006) 'Putting staff wellbeing higher on the agenda', *Independent Education*, 36(3):20–21.

Yoon JS (2002) 'Teacher characteristics as predictors of teacher-student relationships: stress, negative affect, and self-efficacy', *Social Behavior & Personality: An International Journal*, 30(5).

CHAPTER 2

Assessing student wellbeing strengths and needs

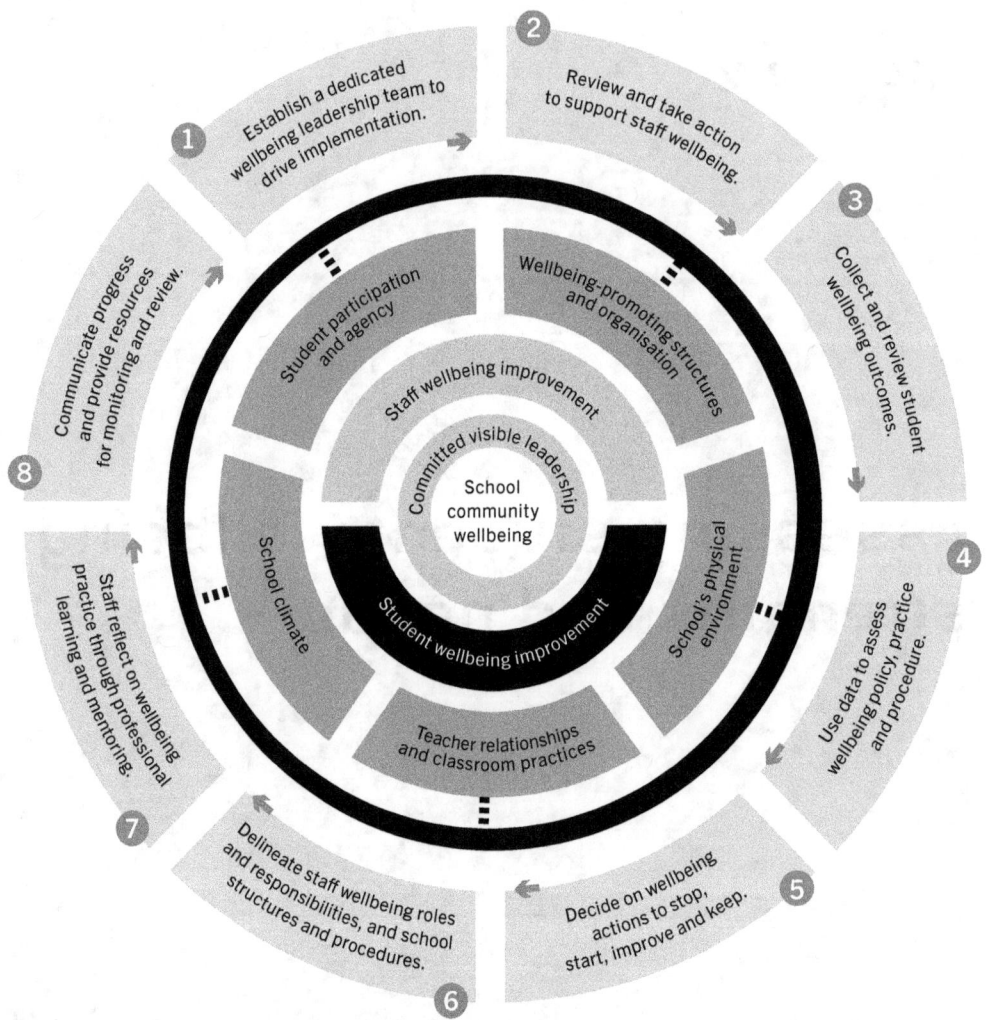

Figure 2.1. Student wellbeing improvement

There are many factors that influence student engagement, performance, achievement and functioning, one of which is student wellbeing. School leaders can provide a welcoming and safe environment where students can flourish and their social and emotional wellbeing needs are met. The impact of the pandemic has highlighted student wellbeing and the importance of schools to monitor the mental health of students. After considering factors that affect student wellbeing, this chapter goes on to describe the importance of and process for establishing a student wellbeing framework, identifying the primary student wellbeing outcomes for schools, the measuring of these outcomes, and translating these findings into policy, procedures and practices to improve student wellbeing.

Factors that affect student wellbeing

A positive state of wellbeing is needed for each student to develop and succeed. Student wellbeing is defined here as a sustainable positive mood and attitude, good health, positive relationships and having the skills and ability to respond effectively to change.

Most schools agree the fundamental purpose of education is the personal, social and academic development of students. Robust evidence shows that personal factors, relationships and school-level factors strongly influence student achievement and positive academic performance and that high student achievement and positive academic performance can also strongly influence student wellbeing. In the past 5–10 years this reciprocal relationship has been more formally recognised at the school and education system level, with the social and emotional development of students seen as critical to the school's mission. However, while the significance of student wellbeing has been broadly recognised and addressed by schools, approaches taken to address student wellbeing have often not been focused, explicit and accountable.

Impacts of the pandemic

There has been widespread concern about the short- and long-term impact of the COVID-19 pandemic on student wellbeing, particularly among vulnerable students such as those experiencing socioeconomic disadvantage (O'Toole and Simovska 2001). The pandemic has exacerbated pre-existing mental health conditions and has increased the prevalence of mental health conditions such as stress and anxiety (Panda et al. 2021). Behavioural symptoms including disruptive behaviours and social interaction difficulties have been associated with pandemic-related isolation and appear to persist as students return to school after shutdown periods (Gore et al. 2021). Given that the long-term effects of the pandemic on mental wellbeing are not known, it is imperative for universal settings like schools to continue to monitor the mental health of children and young people (Lee 2020).

A student's wellbeing reflects their feelings of belonging to their family, peers and school and can affect most aspects of their functioning at school. At the personal level, abilities such as regulating emotions (Thomas 2021), being resilient (Bernard 2004), learning and processing information (Piaget 1968), having positive health and wellbeing (Fatou 2018) and feeling safe (Franklin 2019) all have a significant impact on student learning and engagement.

As discussed in more detail in Chapters 3 and 5, positive relationships between students, teachers and the broader school community and a positive school climate (physical, social and academic) that provides a welcoming and safe environment for learning also significantly influence student achievement (Kutsyuruba et al. 2015). School closures and the move to remote learning during the COVID-19 pandemic highlighted the important role schools play in delivering services and opportunities beyond formal learning. Schools provide safety and protection, links to support services, access to trusted adults, opportunities for play and physical activity, important routines, friendships, health and wellbeing programs and extracurricular activities that all help to build student wellbeing. During school closures, students lose access to these opportunities and the associated social and emotional development, such as building resilience and self-esteem, and emotional and behavioural regulation, with disadvantaged students most affected (O'Toole and Simovska 2001; Flack et al. 2020). Connectedness to school is critical for student wellbeing, with one study showing that 56% of the variance between Year 11 students' self-report of wellbeing was related to how connected they felt to the school (Grazia and Molinari 2021).

The COVID-19 pandemic has presented an opportunity to reflect on the importance of developing respectful and meaningful relationships with families. Families report that home learning has afforded opportunities to better understand the nature of their children's learning. Regular communication and developing mutual trust between school leaders and teachers and families are critical for a positive school climate and positive student outcomes (Emerson et al. 2012).

School climate, academic achievement and mental health

A positive school climate (see Chapter 3) is built through quality school leadership where mutual trust leads to school staff feeling empowered in their positions, which in turn leads to healthy relationships between staff and students. Further, improving relationships between students reduces aggression, bullying and violence, creates a safer and more positive school environment and leads to improvements in student and staff physical and mental health, behavioural and social outcomes, as well as students' academic achievement (Kutsyuruba et al. 2015, Lester and Cross 2015).

Policy and associated procedures at the school level such as behaviour policies can support school safety and therefore academic achievement (Kutsyuruba et al. 2015). At the broader level, academic achievement can be enhanced through community and school partnerships that support student wellbeing, school climate and safety (Kutsyuruba et al. 2015).

It is more important than ever to provide appropriate and relevant resources, with adequate support, to identify and address mental health issues among students. Goldfeld et al. (2022) identified key priority areas to address the indirect impacts of the pandemic on children, including 'expanding the role of schools to address learning gaps and wellbeing' (Goldfeld et al. 2020:364) and 'focusing on prevention and early intervention for mental health' (Goldfeld et al. 2020:368) within education settings. Sonnemann and Goss (2020) have also recommended a strategy for school leadership – the need for a strong focus on wellbeing and social and emotional skill development in teacher education to ensure teachers have the knowledge and the tools to support the wellbeing of their students, identify students who might need additional support and seek help where necessary.

Student wellbeing frameworks

The *Australian Student Wellbeing Framework* (ESA 2018) provides principles to build positive and safe learning environments to support student wellbeing. The 5 key elements (see Figure 2.2) to the framework include:

> Leadership: leaders play an active role in inspiring and creating safe communities and learning environments.

> Inclusion: all school members are involved in building and maintaining inclusive and respectful relationships.

> Student voice: students are authentically engaged in decision-making processes, which will benefit the whole community.

> Partnerships: families and communities engage in effective partnership to support student wellbeing.

> Support: the whole school community understands wellbeing and support for positive behaviour.

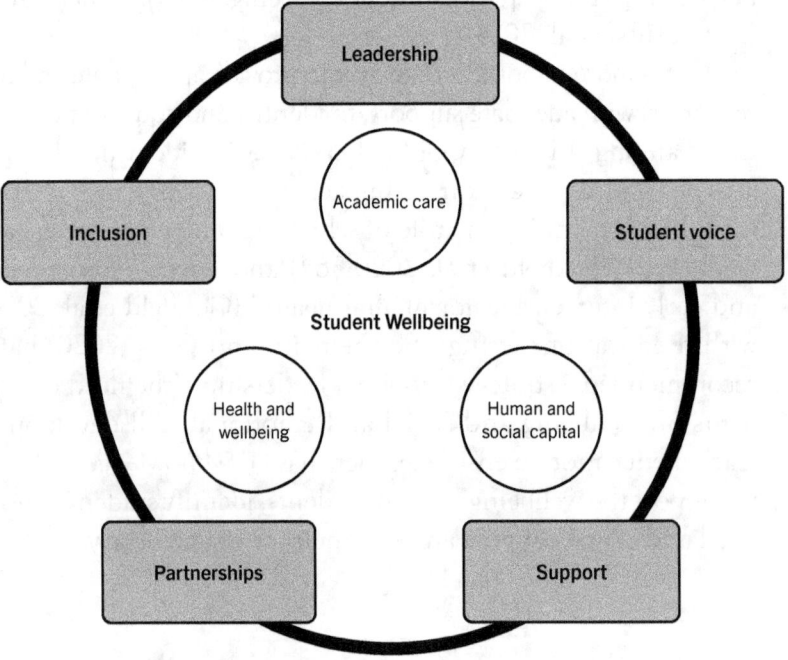

Figure 2.2. Student wellbeing framework elements

Linked to the framework, the *Student Wellbeing Hub* contains the 'School wellbeing check' assessment tool (ESA 2020), which helps schools to identify and analyse school wellbeing within the 5 elements of the framework. The 25 statements within the 'School wellbeing check' ask schools to consider the priority they currently place on wellbeing practices. After survey completion, a report is produced highlighting areas of strengths and areas for improvement and providing feedback for each of the 5 key elements. The survey can be repeated, and the results compared over time. These results can be used to define a student wellbeing framework, with schools considering the policies, procedures, practices and professional development they use to promote and support their students' safety and wellbeing, and to understand the impact these are having on students' wellbeing (and learning). By defining a student wellbeing framework and assessing the performance of the 5 key elements in their school, schools can begin to identify strategies to promote and sustain the wellbeing of the whole school community. This represents the first of the following 4-step high-impact processes discussed in the rest of this chapter:

1. Define a student wellbeing framework
2. Identify student wellbeing outcomes
3. Measure student wellbeing outcomes
4. Interpret, plan and implement

Define a student wellbeing framework

This section describes how to tailor the student wellbeing framework to reflect the needs of the school by providing a worked example. The first task is to identify and define principles for each of the 5 key elements (leadership, inclusion, student voice, partnerships, support). A principle is a statement that defines an overall outcome. For example, within the 'Student voice' element, one principle may be defined as, 'Students are active participants in their own learning and wellbeing, feel connected and use their social and emotional skills to be respectful, resilient, and safe.' For each principle within the 5 key elements, a student wellbeing framework can be populated by clarifying the following 4 questions:

1. What does the school aim to do to address these student wellbeing outcomes? (Aims)
2. What student wellbeing outcomes are planned to be addressed? (Outcomes)
3. What are the indicators of effective policy and practice for student wellbeing? (Indicators)
4. How will these outcomes be assessed and monitored? (Assessment)

The elements of a student wellbeing framework need to have indicators of effective practice at both the whole-school level and the individual level. The impact of school wellbeing processes, structures, policies and procedures on student wellbeing outcomes can be measured and reported at the whole-school level (student, teacher, school) through relationships with staff and peers, classroom management, peer collaboration, engagement, inclusion, student voice, positive beliefs and expectations and teacher–parent/caregiver relationships (Cefai and Cavioni 2013). Figure 2.3 depicts the relationship between elements, principles and practices in a student wellbeing framework.

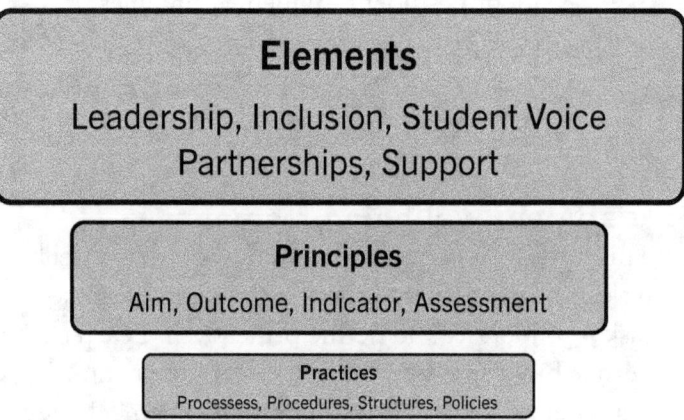

Figure 2.3. Defining a student wellbeing framework

An example of a school wellbeing framework focusing on 'student voice' (as discussed in Chapter 4) is displayed in Table 2.1. This table defines aims, outcomes, indicators at the student, teacher and school level and the underlying practices needed to support the school leadership team.

Table 2.1. Example of a student wellbeing framework focusing on student voice*†

AIMS	OUTCOMES	INDICATORS	MEASUREMENT

• To provide opportunities for student decision-making about things that affect them.
• To create and maintain inclusive and interactive learning environments to encourage student participation and foster connectedness.
• To use evidence-informed, strengths-based approaches to enhance students' learning and wellbeing.
• To explicitly teach social and emotional skills using evidence-informed practices related to personal safety, resilience, help-seeking and protective behaviours.
• To co-develop strategies with students to enhance wellbeing, promote safety and counter violence, bullying and abuse (online and physical).
	• A supportive school environment, with a clear ethos, structure and organisation to ensure student participation.
	• A curriculum that supports and promotes 'academic care' through building 'resiliency', enhancing positive self-efficacy, healthy risk-taking and goal-setting, negotiation, reflection and empowerment; enabling students to reach their full potential.
	• Clear guidelines addressing the roles, responsibilities, training requirements and procedures for the promotion of supportive partnerships with students.
		School level:
		• Clear policies, programs and procedures on school ethos, structure and student welfare are co-developed with students.
		• Leadership promotes student voice and regularly includes students in decision-making.
		• Programs promote peer support, student involvement on decision-making bodies and teacher teams working with student groups.
		
		Teacher level:
		• Teachers foster positive interactions through discussion groups, collaborative work, speaking and listening, questioning, acknowledging viewpoints, justifying positions and fair treatment.
		• Teachers create opportunities for different forms of student contribution.
		• Teachers hone student knowledge of decision-making processes and create student leadership opportunities.
		• Teachers and students agree on classroom rules.
		
		Student level:
		• Leadership opportunities are promoted and training is provided for student leadership teams, including mentoring and peer support.
		• Students have increased opportunities to be recognised for effort and participation.
		• Student and staff connectedness is promoted.
		• Students can participate in school activities, including on boards and committees (e.g. on a student representative council).
		• Students can participate in student-owned and student-directed activities.
			• Attendance, behavioural and academic data
			• Student surveys measuring:
			  › mental, social, emotional, physical and spiritual wellbeing
			  › effectiveness of school policies and structures, such as relationships, engagement, social and emotional skills and school climate
			• Qualitative data collected via focus groups and interviews, to understand what is working well, what could be improved, what needs to stop and what needs to start.

*'Aims' column adapted from ESA (Education Services Australia) (2020) *Your School Wellbeing Check*, Education Council, Carlton South, VIC, used under CC BY 4.0.

† 'Outcomes', 'Indicators' and 'Assessment' columns adapted from Hearn L, Campbell-Pope R, House J, Cross D (2006) *Pastoral care in education*, Child Health Promotion Research Unit, Edith Cowan University, Perth.

Identify student wellbeing outcomes

Student wellbeing is concerned with promoting students' social, emotional, physical, spiritual and academic development and fostering positive attitudes to respond effectively to change and unpredictability. These core outcomes of student wellbeing can be achieved through policies and practices that focus on the promotion of 3 key areas: health and wellbeing, academic care and human and social capital. These areas need to be supported by the 5 student wellbeing framework elements of leadership, inclusion, student voice, partnerships and support.

The results of the school wellbeing check will help identify student wellbeing needs within the school. Within the student wellbeing framework, each element can be linked to student wellbeing outcomes. For example, as shown in Table 2.1, student voice can be linked with social wellbeing outcomes, such as a sense of belonging to school, close relationships with teachers, connectedness to peers, and feeling safe at school. The school's mission, vision and values also often reflect the main goals for student wellbeing outcomes (see Figure 2.4).

Figure 2.4. School values

Many programs run in schools already have identified wellbeing outcomes. For example, anti-bullying, peer-support and mindfulness programs often have outcomes that can be measured and that align with individual student wellbeing domains, such as academic, social and emotional, mental, physical and spiritual wellbeing.

Wellbeing indicators can be useful signs for teachers and school leaders to gauge the success or otherwise of the wellbeing outcomes they are aiming for with their students. Examples of some student wellbeing indicators are presented in Table 2.2.

Table 2.2. Student wellbeing indicators

WELLBEING DOMAINS	WELLBEING INDICATORS				
Academic	Perseverance	Independence	Motivation	Engagement	Attitudes towards school
Social and emotional	School connectedness	Teacher connectedness	Peer social support	Bullying experiences	Loneliness
Mental	Resilience	Life satisfaction	Emotional regulation	Depression	Anxiety
Physical	Physical activity	Screen use	Sleep duration	Sleep quality	Use of alcohol and other drugs
Other	Transition expectations	Transition experience			

Leadership practice idea: case study

The school wellbeing team worked with students to co-design a tailored student wellbeing survey that targeted aspects of the school's wellbeing framework, focusing on academic/intellectual and emotional wellbeing.

By collecting student wellbeing data, the school staff were able to identify what aspects of student wellbeing to target. In this case, the priority was students' academic resilience, linked to their motivation and engagement. While the school offered a broad wellbeing curriculum, staff decided (based on the data collected) to focus on building social and emotional skills for learning and resilience.

The student wellbeing baseline data provided helpful insights into how and which students were experiencing anxiety and stress and, particularly, their vulnerability related to academic risk-taking and resilience.

The school leadership has committed to gathering longitudinal student wellbeing data using the same survey for at least 3 years, to understand trends, to identify the strengths and needs of each year level and to identify who may be experiencing difficulties.

Leadership practice idea: case study

The school leadership team found that embedding a whole-school wellbeing framework takes time and commitment. The school staff identified several areas where wellbeing interconnected with the school system, using a modified version of the model shown in Figure 2.5 developed by Waters (2011a, 2011b, 2012).

Figure 2.5. Leading cultural change at schools through a positive psychology approach

Source: Waters (2011a, 2011b, 2012)

Managing the change process and aligning it with student and staff outcomes required a staged approach with a clear sense of long-term outcomes. Over a 3-year period, the school:

> included wellbeing in the strategic review
> designed a wellbeing framework
> created the role of Head of Wellbeing
> appointed 3 wellbeing assistants to help drive wellbeing strategy/ implement interventions
> developed a new wellbeing curriculum using evidence-based programs for students
> trained staff in the foundations of positive psychology
> commenced a parent education program
> began student wellbeing longitudinal data collection
> undertook a qualitative review of pastoral care
> identified policies that benefited from being viewed through the 'lens of wellbeing'
> overhauled student behaviour management procedures, to move from a model that relies on student compliance and some inconsistent punitive measures towards a positive behaviour approach based on character strengths and virtues associated with self-discipline/self-determination theory/self-leadership.

Measure student wellbeing outcomes

Measuring student wellbeing enables schools to benchmark and monitor student strengths and needs to more effectively target evidence-based policies and practices to improve these student outcomes. This requires the use of valid and reliable tools that measure the various facets of student social, emotional, physical, mental and spiritual wellbeing, which fit within the school's wellbeing framework.

Measuring and tracking student wellbeing can be achieved by answering the following 2 questions:

1. What wellbeing-related data are already collected by the school?
2. How can our school assess wellbeing outcomes that are not being measured?

Leadership practice idea: case study

To review their health and wellbeing program, the leadership team used an annual online survey to collect information about the students' health and wellbeing, resilience, academic care and social capital. The survey included previously tested valid and reliable scales to ask the students about how they feel about themselves and how they feel about their school, friends, mental health, motivation, engagement, family, use of screen time, sleep and transition. These annual surveys are now used to track student health and wellbeing and enable the staff to collect data specific and relevant to the health and wellbeing of their students. Longitudinal comparisons were also made for students who completed the survey over the past four years. These student data are used by staff in conjunction with anecdotal evidence and regular discussions with the school's wellbeing team to guide the health and wellbeing program.

What wellbeing-related data are already collected by the school?

School leaders collect many forms of data as part of their regulatory requirements. These data obviously include academic data, such as student grades, AECD, NAPLAN, VCE, HSC and OLNA results, behavioural data and attendance data. Some school staff supplement these data by using information collected in student surveys measuring the quality of procedures and practices in the school or other outcomes of interest such as student attitudes, specific behaviours like alcohol and drug use or technology use, or program outcome surveys, as well as staff and parent surveys. These data can be used to track individual students or to understand more specifically how well different structures in the school are functioning, such as wellbeing delivery through year levels or houses. Schools can use these data to benchmark, monitor and review current policy and practices to ensure they meet the school community needs and to plan for universal, indicated or targeted interventions, programs or services. Importantly, school leaders could also try to access data collected by school systems.

How can wellbeing outcomes that are not being measured be assessed?

Student wellbeing outcomes can be hard to measure because they need to be defined precisely and it can be difficult to isolate the specific influences of the home and school environments on students' wellbeing. Both qualitative and quantitative data collection methods can be used to measure and review student wellbeing outcomes. Qualitative methods such as interviews and focus groups can be used to provide a comprehensive understanding of what structures, systems, curriculum, policies and procedures in the school are supportive of student wellbeing. Qualitative data can also be used to gather in-depth information from students, staff and parents to help understand what is working well, what needs to be improved or stopped and what is missing to support student wellbeing. Some examples of the types of qualitative findings schools have used to inform process, policies and procedures are provided in the case studies below.

Leadership practice idea: case study

Student data collected in this school through surveys found that the major concerns for students occurred during their transition from primary to secondary school. Many reported they were worried they would get lost and would not be able to find classrooms. In response, school staff posted maps around the school, included a walk-around of the main classrooms on orientation day and established an older buddy system for other students to meet new students on the first day to help them find their way around.

Also, students in this school reported through the surveys that the only contact they had with their head of house, who was primarily responsible for student wellbeing, was negative. They indicated the only time they spent with the head of house was discussing behavioural, attendance and uniform issues. As a result of this finding,

> school staff encouraged student leaders to help with uniform regulation, allowing the heads of house to have more positive interactions with students.
>
> This school survey also identified some barriers to students seeing a school counsellor, mainly because they felt they didn't know the counsellors and because of the perceived stigma associated with seeing them. To reduce stigma, school staff responded by giving counsellors time during the year to informally engage, get to know and build relationships with students through informal homeroom class visits, extra-curricular activities, camps and while walking around the school grounds during break times.

Quantitative student wellbeing data are typically collected by schools using hard copy or online surveys where the data can be collected anonymously or confidentially, depending on whether school staff want to track student wellbeing cases over time. Reliable and validated scales need to be used to measure student wellbeing outcomes, with results compared to age and gender norms where these are available; for example, Strengths and Difficulties Questionnaire (SDQ) for psychological attributes such as emotional symptoms, conduct problems, hyperactivity, peer relationship problems and prosocial behaviour (Youthinmind 2022) and The Motivation and Engagement Scale (Lifelong Achievement Group 2022). Scales measuring different student wellbeing outcomes can be used to collect data at both the school and student level and need to include demographics such as year level, gender and house to allow comparisons to be made within the school.

Quantitative surveys can be used both cross-sectionally and longitudinally to track wellbeing in student cohorts and within students over time (see Figure 2.6). Cross-sectional data provide a snapshot of a point in time, allowing for comparisons between year levels, whereas longitudinal data allow for tracking of students between and within cohorts over time. For longitudinal data, student identifiers need to be collected so these data can be linked to school-held data (academic, behavioural, attendance, service use) and to enable staff to monitor students over time. Longitudinal collection of student data can also be used to monitor student academic and health and wellbeing trajectories and to identify school- and student-level predictors of wellbeing. For example, if practices are implemented to increase social wellbeing by reducing bullying, the school wellbeing team may also measure social outcomes over time by linking these data to student behavioural and attendance records. These analyses would allow the school to assess the effectiveness of the anti-bullying program on student behaviour and attendance.

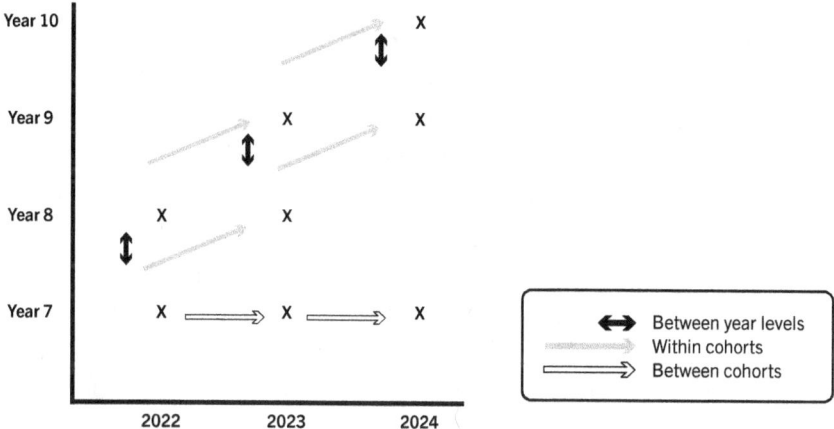

Figure 2.6. Tracking wellbeing cross-sectionally and longitudinally

There are many standardised surveys that can be used to measure wellbeing outcomes, but surveys need to be tailored to measure each school's student wellbeing needs and outcomes. Some examples of standardised surveys include the Social–Emotional Wellbeing survey (ACER 2023) and the Be You (2023b) survey tool, which measures student wellbeing and the school environment.

Leadership practice idea: case study

School staff conducted a qualitative pastoral care review to provide an in-depth review of school structures, systems, practices and procedures to determine ways they could alleviate the increasing levels of stress and anxiety they noticed in some of their students. The school leadership team used these data to identify what school actions could be taken organisationally, such as with the allied health team in conjunction with implementing programs like *Be You* (2023a) and *Friendly Schools* (2023) to help enhance student wellbeing.

Schools need effective data collection and storage systems that protect privacy and allow for the identification, monitoring and reporting on student behaviour and wellbeing. These systems need a dashboard that enables staff to extract data, in ways that can be understood and used to support and promote the wellbeing of students effectively and efficiently.

Interpret, plan and implement

While school leaders have access to (or collect) substantial student behaviour and wellbeing data, some report they do not have the specific knowledge or skills to use these data to provide deep insight, to determine and to tailor their school's response. These findings for example, can be interpreted at the whole-school level, at different house or year levels and at the individual student level.

Findings on student wellbeing need to be interpreted carefully. Student demographics need to be considered, as the data are only representative of the students involved in data collection. For example, there may be a group of students who were unable to participate in the data collection, such as students with low attendance or students who have English as a second language, who also need to be considered in the delivery of the school's response. Findings may also be limited by:

> - what is measured; for example, if the survey focuses only on deficits or strengths instead of both
> - measuring only specific wellbeing outcomes that do not address all student wellbeing needs
> - the validity and reliability of the scales used.

Key school staff often require professional learning to enhance their knowledge and ability to collect and analyse data, and the skills to interpret and integrate evidence-based decisions and recommendations that respond to student wellbeing needs. Trained support is often also needed to help school staff identify the most applicable survey items and scales and to collect and interpret the data for school wellbeing action.

Actions based on findings

Student wellbeing outcome data will help to provide evidence of the effectiveness of the actions the school staff are taking formally and informally to address student wellbeing. In contrast, process or administration data describing how systems and initiatives are being used, by whom, when and for how long, and how staff and students (and parents if the data are collected) are feeling about these initiatives will provide evidence towards the impact of the initiatives. Hence, both the outcome data and the process data provide ideas to help school staff make evidence-based decisions to target student wellbeing policies and practices more effectively.

Involving students and staff when interpreting the data is an effective way to increase their understanding of student wellbeing and ownership of subsequent actions. Some schools present and workshop the data with staff to identify and prioritise recommended actions and their implementation. Subgroups of parents can also be involved in this process to seek their recommendations and engagement in the proposed actions.

Leadership practice idea: case study

The school leadership team used the findings from their student wellbeing data collection to identify several areas of concern. Using one of their professional development days, the leadership team presented the data and gathered feedback on what actions the school staff thought were needed to respond to these data. Groups of staff were each given butcher's paper and some leadership recommendations and tasked with reviewing and prioritising the recommendations (short-term and long-term). Each group then displayed their recommendations in ranked order and all staff were invited to vote on which recommendations they thought were the most important. The top 3 recommendations were identified and the afternoon was spent in staff groups identifying ways to implement the recommendations.

It will also be important for the school wellbeing team to identify students whose wellbeing may be at-risk and in need of targeted support (see Chapter 4). Most schools have policies or formal mechanisms to identify higher need students and processes in place to work with parents of students experiencing difficulties. Close affiliations and established partnerships with community services are also needed to ensure strong referral systems to community-based health and allied health professionals, such as social workers, youth workers, clinical psychologists and mental health agencies. Some school leaders have also invited allied health services onto the campus as regular itinerant service providers or, in some instances, have provided space on the school grounds to establish clinical services for young people and their families.

Further staff professional learning is often identified as an outcome of a student wellbeing review to build teachers' capacity to monitor, grow and support students' social and emotional wellbeing. Identifying quality training providers can be challenging; however, education systems in most states offer evidence-based professional learning and resources in social and emotional learning, with some other organisations offering evidence-based social and emotional toolkits and online training.

The promotion of student wellbeing through the development of a student wellbeing framework requires strong leadership. As indicated in Figure 2.7, defining principles for each key element need to be mapped to the student wellbeing framework, with the aims, outcomes, indicators and assessment of each principle defined. The outcomes from policy, procedures and programs need to be measured across the whole school and with this evidence base, decisions and recommendations can be made around supporting student wellbeing. Professional development in identifying, measuring and interpreting student wellbeing outcomes may be required. Actions include targeting resources, identifying at-risk students and implementing policy change. Identification of key priorities, evidence-based policies and programs and the development of a clear plan of implementation and delivery leads to structural or policy change intended to support student wellbeing. Once changes are made, the impact is regularly measured to ensure the changes are having the intended result.

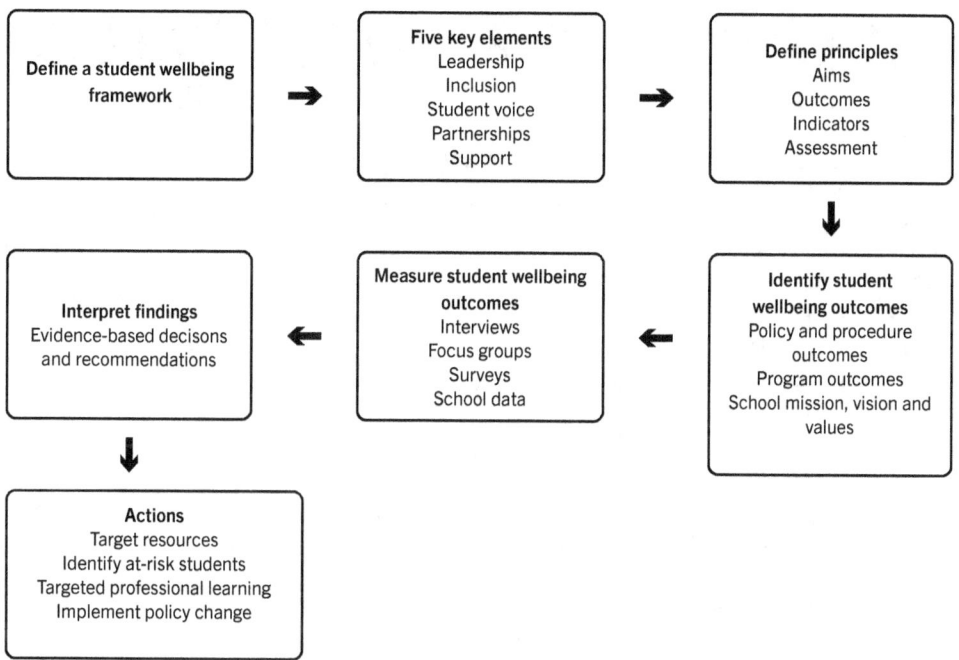

Figure 2.7. Promotion of student wellbeing processes

Chapter summary

This chapter outlines the factors affecting student wellbeing and the importance of developing a student wellbeing framework to assess, benchmark and monitor the wellbeing strengths and needs of students. The student wellbeing framework aims to help school staff identify and analyse student wellbeing data based on school values and the priority they place on wellbeing practices to improve overall student wellbeing. The case studies provide examples of how schools have designed a student wellbeing framework, measured student wellbeing outcomes, made evidence-based decisions based on their findings and how they have taken action to target student wellbeing policies and practices. The following checklist can be used to review high-impact practices needed to determine, assess and improve student wellbeing outcomes.

To determine, assess and improve student wellbeing outcomes we:	Not in place	Working towards	In place	Progressing well
Provide professional learning opportunities for staff to build their capacity to monitor and implement actions that respond to student wellbeing data findings.				
Identify relevant community agencies to refer and provide support to students identified as experiencing wellbeing difficulties.				
Collect, assess, monitor and review student wellbeing data annually.				
Appoint a student wellbeing committee to lead the process to determine student wellbeing outcomes, their measurement and actions taken because of the findings.				
Develop and use a student wellbeing framework to guide our data collection and decision-making processes.				
Clearly define the student wellbeing outcomes prioritised by the school community.				
Use student wellbeing data to enable the whole school community to understand, prioritise and take action to support student wellbeing.				
Use student wellbeing data to determine actions to build and maintain safe, inclusive and respectful relationships.				
Authentically engage students in the wellbeing outcome data collection and decision-making processes related to identifying student wellbeing priorities.				
Authentically engage families in the student wellbeing outcome data collection, interpretation and decision-making to identify student wellbeing priorities.				
Use data to enhance allied health and other school services to support higher risk students and those experiencing difficulties.				

References

ACER (Australian Council for Educational Research) (2023) *Social–Emotional Wellbeing Survey*, ACER website, accessed 26 January 2023. https://www.acer.org/au/sew

Benard B (2004) *Resiliency: what we have learned*, WestEd, San Francisco, CA.

Be You (2023a) *BeYou* [website], accessed 26 January 2023. https://beyou.edu.au/

Be You (2023b) *Planning and Implementation Tools*, BeYou website, accessed 26 January 2023. https://beyou.edu.au/planning-and-implementation-tools

Cefai C, Cavioni V (2013) *Social and emotional education in primary school: integrating theory and research into practice*, Springer, New York.

Emerson L, Fear J, Fox S, Sanders E (2012) *Parental engagement in learning and schooling: lessons from research*, a report by the Australian Research Alliance for Children and Youth (ARACY) for the Family–School and Community Partnerships Bureau, Canberra.

ESA (Education Services Australia) (2018) *Australian Student Wellbeing Framework*, Education Council, Carlton South, VIC, accessed 17 January 2023. https://studentwellbeinghub.edu.au/educators/framework

ESA (Education Services Australia) (2020) *Your School Wellbeing Check*, Education Council, Carlton South, VIC, accessed 26 January 2023. https://studentwellbeinghub.edu.au/educators/framework

Fatou N, Kubiszewski V (2018) 'Are perceived school climate dimensions predictive of students' engagement?' *Soc. Psychol. Educ.*, 21:427–446 doi: 10.1007/s11218-017-9422-x.

Flack CB, Walker L, Bickerstaff A, Earle H, Margetts C (2020) *Educator perspectives on the impact of COVID-19 on teaching and learning in Australia and New Zealand*, Pivot Professional Learning, Melbourne, Australia.

Franklin H, Harrington I (2019) 'A review into effective classroom management and strategies for student engagement: teacher and student roles in today's classrooms', *Journal of Education and Training Studies*, 7(12):1–12.

Friendly Schools (2023) *Friendly Schools* [website], accessed 26 January. https://friendlyschools.com.au/

Goldfeld S, O'Connor E, Sung V, Roberts G, Wake M, West S, Hiscock H (2022) 'Potential indirect impacts of the COVID-19 pandemic on children: a narrative review using a community child health lens', *Medical Journal of Australia*, 216(7):364–372.

Gore J, Fray L, Miller A, Harris J, Taggart W (2021) 'The impact of COVID-19 on student learning in New South Wales primary schools: an empirical study', *The Australian Educational Researcher*, 48:605–637.

Grazia V, Molinari L (2021) 'School climate multidimensionality and measurement: A systematic literature review', *Research Papers in Education*, 36(5):561–587.

Kutsyuruba B, Klinger DA, Hussain A (2015) 'Relationships among school climate, school safety, and student achievement and well-being: a review of the literature', *Review of Education*, 3(2):103–135.

Lee J (2020) 'Mental health effects of school closures during COVID-19', *The Lancet Child & Adolescent Health*, 4(6):421.

Lester L, Cross D (2015) 'The relationship between school climate and mental and emotional wellbeing over the transition from primary to secondary school', *Psychology of Well-Being*, 5(1):1.

Lifelong Achievement Group (2022) *The Motivation and Engagement Scale (MES)*, Lifelong Achievement Group website, accessed 26 January 2023. https://lifelongachievement.com/pages/the-motivation-and-engagement-scale-mes

O'Toole C, Simovska V (2001) 'Same storm, different boats! The impact of COVID-19 on the wellbeing of school communities', *Health Education*.

Panda PK, Gupta J, Chowdhury SR, Kumar R, Meena AK, Madaan P, Sharawat IK, Gulati S (2021) 'Psychological and behavioral impact of lockdown and quarantine measures for COVID-19 pandemic on children, adolescents and caregivers: a systematic review and meta-analysis', *Journal of Tropical Pediatrics*, 67(1):fmaa122.

Piaget J (1968) *Six psychological studies* (A Tenzer, trans.), Vintage Books, New York.

Sonnemann J, Goss P (2020) *COVID catch-up: helping disadvantaged students close the equity gap*, Grattan Institute.

Thomas CL, Allen K (2021) `Driving engagement: investigating the influence of emotional intelligence and academic buoyancy on student engagement', *Journal of Further and Higher Education*, 45(1):107–119.

Waters L (2011a) 'A review of school-based positive psychology interventions', *Australian Educational and Developmental Psychologist*, 28(2):75–90.

Waters L (2011b) 'Building positive psychology into a new School Leader's program in Victoria', *Australian Association for Educational Researchers*, Nov 27–Dec 1, Hobart.

Waters L (2012) 'Whole of school approach to positive psychology: how do you do it?' *South Australian Government Premier and Cabinet Wellbeing before Learning Conference*, Adelaide Convention Centre, February 27, Adelaide.

Youthinmind (2022) *SDQ: Information for researchers and Professionals about the Strengths & Difficulties Questionnaires*, sdqinfo.org website, accessed 26 January 2023. https://www.sdqinfo.org/

Part 2

What's needed?

Actions for continuous improvement for school community wellbeing

CHAPTER 3

Taking school community wellbeing from good to great: getting the climate right

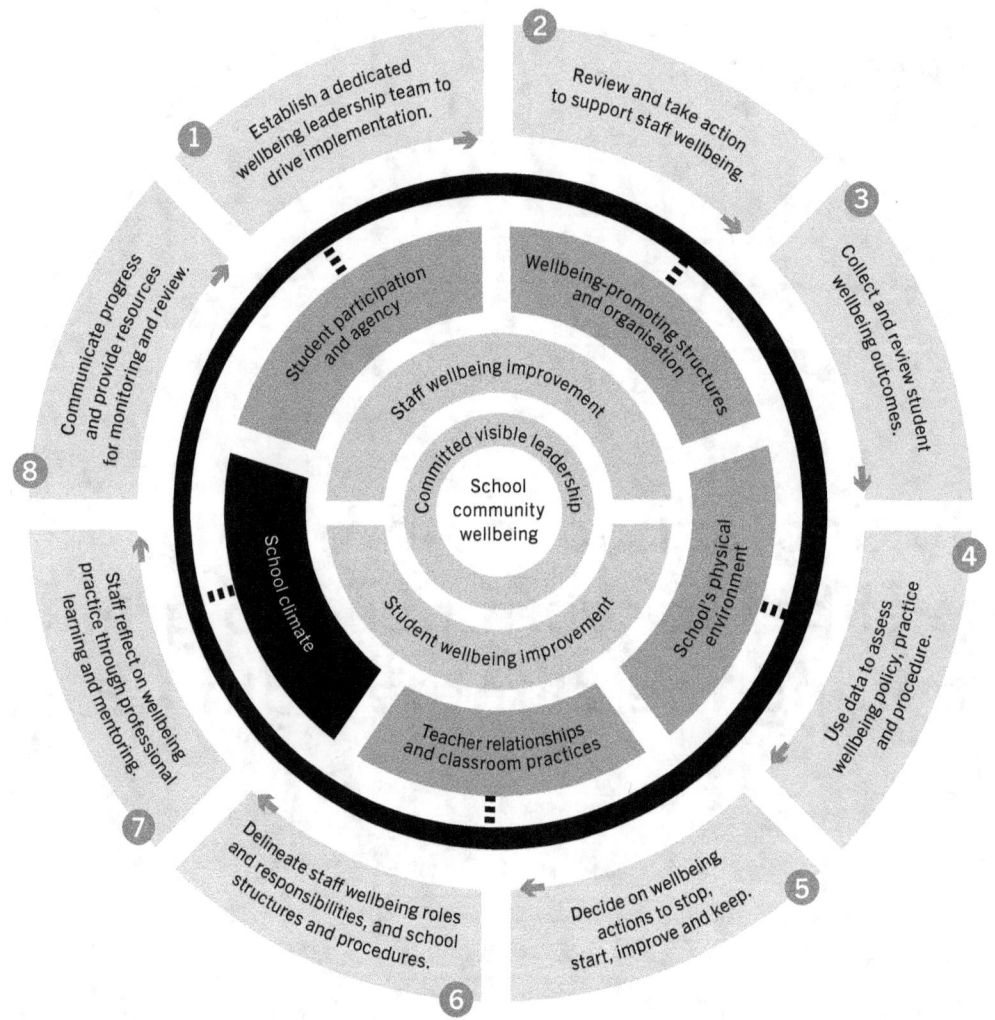

Figure 3.1. School climate

School climate *really* matters ...

School climate is the precursor for and consequence of the school community's commitment to:

> promoting a supportive academic, disciplinary and physical environment

> fostering a sense of school connectedness, belonging and perceptions of safety

> encouraging and enabling respectful, trusting, caring, inclusive and supportive relationships throughout the school community, including with families.

School climate is often described as the 'quality and character of school life' and is essentially 'the effect of the school on its community'. Some equate building a school's climate to creating conditions for student learning, where students are supported, socially capable, safe and challenged (Aldridge and McChesney 2018).

School leaders can create a virtuous (or vicious) cycle for their school climate. Kutsyuruba et al. (2015) found that principals impact the climate of the school because they are largely responsible for building trust – the foundation of all relationships – and they do this through their leadership style. School climate doesn't just appear or exist; it must be made, embedded and maintained through school leadership.

This chapter describes the importance and critical responsibility of school leaders to establish and sustain a positive school climate that sets the tone and expectations for the school community's behaviour, which subsequently affects their wellbeing.

While the influence of school climate on students' learning is well documented (Bradshaw et al. 2014), the extent of its profound impact on the social, emotional and cognitive development and wellbeing of both students and staff has only recently become more deeply understood (Bradshaw et al. 2014).

Much research has found that school leaders impact student achievement and outcomes (Coelli and Green 2012; Day et al. 2016; Grissom et al. 2019; Grissom et al. 2015; Klusmann et al. 2016, Leithwood et al. 2018) by enabling supportive school learning environments that focus on:

> developing relationships

> quality culturally responsive teaching and learning

> inquiry-based learning

> enhanced teacher morale, satisfaction and capacity

> positive professional development

> positive parent and community collaboration.

Quality leadership also impacts school climate by enhancing teachers' motivation and students' academic success (Day et al. 2016, Riley 2013). Conversely, principal turnover negatively affects student achievement (Bartanen et al. 2019) and ineffective leadership limits student outcomes (Grissom et al. 2019). Unsurprisingly, school leaders – through their influence on their school's climate and their staff – significantly impact the students' learning environments and academic outcomes (Coelli and Green 2012) as well as the whole school community's wellbeing.

Defining school climate

Terms including 'school culture' or 'school ethos' are sometimes used to describe this school-level group phenomenon. For this chapter, the term 'school climate' encapsulates both 'school culture' and 'school ethos'. School climate (as distinct from 'classroom climate' discussed in Chapter 4) is defined as:

> *The shared values, beliefs, norms, behaviours, expectations and traditions unique to a school that it accepts and promotes, and that therefore pervade all aspects of school life, influencing how it functions. (Deal and Peterson 2010)*

School climate is affected by the kinds of relationships that exist within the whole school community: feelings of inclusivity, wellbeing, safety, and the presence of support, where school staff are aware of and respond to their students' strengths and needs. It includes a shared vision of policies and practices that focus on building trust, respect, connectedness, support, positive attitudes to diversity and inclusion and less bullying. School climate also sets the tone for behaviours that are considered acceptable and normative for members of the school community (Kuperminc et al. 1997).

An assessment of the whole-school climate is typically based on the school community's collective perceptions and experiences of the interactions between students, teachers and families and:

> teaching and learning practices

> organisational structures

> safety

> physical environment. (Cohen et al. 2009)

While teachers typically focus more on their classroom-level climate, students are more sensitive to school-level factors – clearly indicating that a whole-school approach to improving school climate is essential (Thapa et al. 2013).

School climate is critical, as students' perceptions and experiences of school life influence their:

> social, emotional and cognitive development (including academic achievement)

> feelings of engagement, respect and care (As discussed in Chapter 4, students' social and emotional development, mental and physical health and connectedness to school are significantly enhanced when they experience positive, trusting, cooperative and caring relationships with school staff) (Rutledge et al. 2015; Tichnor-Wagner and Allen 2016)

> feelings of social, emotional and physical safety (Klein et al. 2012).

What is the effect of a positive school climate?

Variations in a school's climate, especially the social and emotional tone, can lead to significant differences in student wellbeing, behaviour and achievement. Growing evidence links school climate to students' improved psychosocial wellbeing, including their self-esteem and ability to resolve conflict, motivation to strive academically and ability to engage in altruistic and prosocial behaviour (Bradshaw et al. 2014; Coelli and Green 2012; Day et al. 2016; Grissom et al. 2019; Grissom et al. 2015).

An inverse and synergistic relationship between school climate and risky student behaviours exists; as school climate improves, risky behaviours such as bullying typically decrease, which ameliorates the school's climate. A positive school climate where students feel safe, respected and supported is the best predictor of school satisfaction for adolescents, followed by relationships between teachers and students (Wang et al. 2020). When it is working well, school climate can help mitigate the impact of a low socioeconomic background on students' academic achievement (Berkowitz et al. 2017) and can significantly and positively influence rates of student absenteeism, truancy, drop-out (Klusmann et al. 2016), suspension (Bertanen et al. 2019), bullying behaviour and drug use (Bradshaw et al. 2014), as well as teacher turnover.

Klein et al. (2012) found that positive teacher–student relationships, improved behavioural support, and fair and clear rules and expectations can significantly reduce youth involvement in antisocial behaviours, and that these factors explain 66% of the variance in risky behaviours between schools. If students regularly experience trusted, respectful, responsive and caring relationships with school staff, they are more likely to take action to care for or help others and respond compassionately to aggression and bullying (Konishi et al. 2021). These behaviours can positively influence norms, reducing pressure on and need for school staff alone to quell poor behaviour. Student 'upstanding' action, for example, can reduce bullying behaviour faster and for a more sustained period, than action solely from teachers. This student action does not mitigate staff responsibility, but instead demonstrates a whole-school behavioural expectation that all school community members share the responsibility for keeping the school safe.

Affirming cultural diversity as part of a positive school climate is also associated with fewer social problems, like bullying perpetration, victimisation (Thapa et al. 2013) and other aggressive and violent behaviour (Bradshaw et al. 2014). School leaders need to ensure normative standards, rules and processes are in place to prevent prejudice behaviour and to enable students to be inclusive and fair, to act to help and to report prejudice behaviour they become aware of.

School climate can also affect school improvement and change processes, through the quality of the relationships and collaboration between staff and their relationships with and between students (Thapa et al. 2013). School improvement reforms are more likely to be implemented and successful, for example, when they are closely aligned with a positive school climate (Deal and Peterson 1999).

How to assess and monitor school climate

Identifying multiple pathways to enhance students' academic performance, such as through a positive school climate, helps staff use actions beyond simply more effective instruction (Zullig and Matthews-Ewald 2014), which, while necessary, may not be sufficient on its own to reduce gaps in student achievement.

Chapter 2 describes ways school leaders can assess student wellbeing, to help determine and monitor specific staff actions required to respond to local needs or the impact of circumstances (such as the impact of a major bushfire, flood or pandemic) on students' wellbeing. However, these individual wellbeing assessments may need to be supplemented with collective or school community-level measures of school climate. An example of a quality school climate measure developed for Australian students is the What's Happening in this School? (WHITS) questionnaire (Aldridge and Ala'I 2013), using scales measuring teacher support, peer connectedness and school connectedness.

As students and staff experience school climate differently, it is essential to assess how each group perceive they are influenced by the school's academic, social, emotional and built environment. This assessment needs to involve respondents who are representative of the whole school community, all age groups of students, their teachers and families and other non-teaching school staff and school leaders.

As part of their accountability and continuous improvement systems, school leaders can use school climate data to:

> benchmark their school's climate as perceived by students and staff

> assess student and staff needs and strengths by identifying areas that require improvement

> monitor emerging trends and their effect on student achievement and wellbeing outcomes

> evaluate the effectiveness of actions taken by the school.

Components of an effective school climate

The first and most effective means through which to continuously improve the school climate is to engage the whole school. As we will discuss in Chapter 5, engaging student voice and involving staff, and where possible parents, in action to improve the school climate increases their sense of belonging to the school and the relevancy and ownership of their actions to the whole school community. For example, while school bullying occurs typically between small groups of students, its presence negatively affects the school climate, highlighting the need to engage the whole school in actions to reduce its impact.

Hoy and Hannum (1997) found that the most important school climate variables affecting learning achievement, even after controlling for socioeconomic status (SES), include a focused and orderly learning environment (academic emphasis), teachers showing much commitment to their students (teacher affiliation) and adequate supply and material support for teaching (resource support).

Cohen et al. (2009) identified 7 school-specific components of an effective school climate (in addition to curriculum). They found that these components are most closely associated with positive student academic achievement and improvements in primary and secondary students' psychosocial wellbeing and prosocial behaviour. These components are:

1. Teacher–student and student–student relationships in a culture of equity and fairness (see Chapter 4)
2. The school community's perception of the social, emotional and physical safety of the school (see Chapters 1 and 2)
3. The students' level of school connectedness, engagement and participation (see Chapters 1 and 2)
4. The school's academic care and focus on social and emotional learning (see Chapter 4)
5. The school's physical environment (including facilities) (see Chapter 7)
6. The school's organisation and order (see Chapter 5)
7. The school's behavioural expectations and policy (see Chapter 5).

Strong evidence suggests that improving all 7 of these practices will enhance how students and others in the school community perceive the school climate. However, along with involving the whole school community, the first 4 of the listed components (i.e. teacher–student and student–student relationships in a culture of equity and fairness; the school community's perception of the social, emotional and physical safety of the school; students' level of school connectedness, engagement and participation; the school's academic care and focus on learning) were found by Zullig et al. (2014) to have the greatest effect on students' mental health and wellbeing, especially for secondary students.

The remainder of this chapter discusses evidence-based examples of actions school leaders can implement to improve school climate via these 7 components, plus the engagement of families.

1. Teacher–student and student–student relationships in a culture of equity and fairness

Building supportive structures and processes that shape student and staff attachment and trust and enable continuity in teacher–student relationships are critical to establishing and maintaining these relationships. Some whole-school examples of these structures include learning communities' teaching teams, vertical 'house' groupings that follow students as they progress through years, or other forms of teacher 'looping' (discussed in Chapter 6) to enable longer term relationships between students and teachers (i.e. for more than one year). These structures also help build consistency in practices and predictability in routines, which increase physical, emotional and identity safety. They also encourage a sense of belonging and purpose, reduce student anxiety and support engaged learning.

In addition to organisational structures, leaders need to enable and encourage staff to actively build meaningful teacher–student relationships, such as encouraging staff to get to know and greet students by name. For example, some school leaders encourage staff to use each of their breaktime duty times to learn at least one student's name, including something unique about them. This 'banking of relationship credit' is helpful for staff and students who are experiencing difficulties. Further details on building student wellbeing through teacher relationships are given in Chapter 4.

Ensuring organisational and other actions are culturally and economically responsive, such as creating culturally safe places (informed by the student and parent voices of all cultural groups) and using language that values inclusivity, like 'we' and 'our' rather than 'you' and 'they', will help ensure students feel valued and free from stereotypes that can increase stress and undermine performance. Engaging with all school community members to investigate and acknowledge school-specific values and norms is essential. This can include conducting ongoing self-assessment audits and feedback from students and staff to engage in a reflective process to challenge norms.

Some research suggests significant race-based differences in students' views of school climate (Voight 2015). Many school improvement practices related to school climate, such as giving students a voice or providing individualised care for students, may be vulnerable to inequitable distribution. School leaders need to ensure school climate actions are inclusive of all students of all backgrounds, especially given research showing tacit bias associated with teachers' negative treatment of different cultural groups (Okonofua and Eberhardt 2015).

Leadership practice idea: case study

The principal of a low socioeconomic status and culturally diverse secondary school (54 different nationalities) wanted to understand how students felt about the school climate. Students along with other members of the school community were invited to provide their feedback about what was needed to improve the school climate, as an early step in their school improvement process. Over an 18-month period, the school focused on bringing the members of the school together and implementing the changes that had the support of the whole school community. The process included a collective exercise to re-vision the culture of the school. The most important changes involved increasing teachers' intercultural competence and understanding of living with poverty, using professional learning communities. Teachers used the training to work together to foster an ethos of inclusivity and cultural sensitivity at the school. The principal also wanted to determine the impact of these student-informed school climate actions on students' perceptions of the school climate and their wellbeing, resilience and identity. At the end of the 18-month period, the findings showed students' perceptions of the school climate were significantly higher for 4 of the 6 school climate scales used. Students' self-report mean scores for wellbeing, resilience, self-anchoring and moral identity had also increased significantly.

2. The school community's perception of the school's social, emotional and physical safety

Poor school safety (even students' perceptions of poor school safety) can harm students' wellbeing, school engagement and academic outcomes. Interestingly, students' overall and essential need to feel safe is the most fundamental issue affecting school climate and can be particularly influenced by students' perceptions of school bullying and drug use (Bradshaw et al. 2014). Adults typically overestimate students' perceptions of safety, so school leaders need to invest time to genuinely understand how safe students feel at school. Determining student perceptions of safety is especially important for boys, who consistently report feeling less safe at school than girls (Thapa et al. 2013).

School policies need to form part of other whole-school efforts to establish a school climate that discourages aggressive and other antisocial behaviour, by focussing on building positive relationships between students, their peers and school staff, ensuring consistent responses to bullying incidents, encouraging help-seeking and developing students' social and emotional regulation skills (Wang et al. 2013).

Co-designing behavioural expectations policies with students increases their relevancy, appropriateness and understandability, ensures inclusivity and representation (student voice), encourages compliance and impacts on students' perceived sense of safety (Cross et al. 2015; Mitra 2004). These behavioural policies could encompass issues, such as bullying prevention, that focus on behaviour-learning support and not just discipline, and policies that explicitly prohibit gender and sexual discrimination (Hall 2017). In addition, mapping and modifying the school's physical environment to understand 'hot spots' (see ideas for this in Chapter 7) that affect some students' feelings of safety ensures even the youngest students feel seen and heard.

This collaborative process also enables students to understand and appreciate that school safety is not merely harm prevention but encompasses confidentiality, consent and recognising and responding to signs of antisocial behaviour. Further, providing clear policies that are well understood and easily accessible to school staff, students and families creates known boundaries and facilitates consistent action throughout the whole school community, particularly in relation to methods for help-seeking, rule clarity, rule enforcement and reporting and intervening in safety incidents such as bullying. Promoting upstanding behaviours within the school community enforces school rules and 'perceived fairness'.

Developing school-wide norms and supports for safe, culturally secure and responsive classroom communities provides students with a sense of physical and psychological safety, affirmation and belonging and opportunities to learn social, emotional and cognitive skills.

3. The students' level of school connectedness, engagement and participation

Supporting student engagement in learning enables students to:

> feel they are treated fairly

> develop caring relationships

- seek help
- feel encouraged and challenged to do their best
- set realistic standards
- feel empowered to take part in and contribute to their communities.

Offering and embedding school-wide events that increase perceptions of school connectedness can impact students' sense of belonging and attachment to the school; for example, encouraging student and staff participation in cross-age group and extracurricular activities. Family engagement and broader community involvement is also essential to improve connectedness and participation and their involvement influences school climate. Enabling student and parent voice and involvement (especially among under-represented groups) in school decision-making, such as policy development and rule setting, ensures students are active participants and parents are more likely to be partners in student learning. It is important for students to see their parents engaged and working together, with school staff noticing their effort and helping them feel safer and supported at school. This engagement with families as part of a school improvement process can include:

- seeking feedback, such as that collected via online surveys (e.g. input for school climate improvement), and other positive actions like home visits
- flexibly scheduled student–teacher–parent conferences to learn from parents about their children
- outreach to involve families in school activities
- regular communication through positive phone calls, emails and text messages.

As discussed in more detail below, frequent positive communication also enhances perceptions of connectedness, engagement and participation of all family members.

Broader community partnerships can also help to provide a referral system to external providers for students with health needs beyond the capacity of the school. These partnerships, especially with allied health providers, can also ensure integrated student developmental supports are available to promote students' physical health, mental health and social welfare, through community school models or community partnerships, coupled with family engagement and restorative justice practices.

4. The school's academic care and focus on social and emotional learning

School climate is directly related to student academic achievement (Jones and Shindler 2017). Academic environments with a strong learning and effort focus (versus high demands) are associated with a reduced prevalence of both mental health issues and risk behaviours (Kasen et al. 2009). Creating multi-tiered systems of academic, health and social supports, beginning with universal designs for learning and personalised teaching, and continuing through more intensive academic and non-academic supports, ensures students receive assistance when needed, without labelling or delays. Providing individualised supports and access to integrated services (including physical and mental health and social service supports) by directly responding to student needs addresses potential learning barriers and enables healthy social and emotional development.

Support and structure in the classroom are provided by teacher care, mutual respect, consistent rules and expectations, a clear academic and curricula rationale as well as a rationale for learning – including many opportunities for small group instructional activities (see Chapter 4 for more details). This can also be achieved through providing productive instructional strategies and extended learning opportunities that nurture positive relationships, support motivation, self-efficacy, enrichment and mastery learning (i.e. teaching to help all students achieve a required level of knowledge or skills, before teaching them subsequent knowledge or skills) and help to close achievement gaps.

School staff can ensure teaching practices increase prosocial behaviour by making them sequenced, active, focused and explicit

– 'SAFE'. These 4 social and emotional teaching practices identified in Durlak et al.'s (2011) meta-analyses were found to be associated with significant improvement in students' prosocial behaviour (e.g. cooperation, helping others):

> Sequenced: a connected and coordinated set of activities to foster skill development

> Active: active forms of learning to help students master new skills

> Focused: specific practices devoted to developing personal and social skills

> Explicit: targeted skills clearly identified so students know what is expected of them.

Implementing social and emotional learning (SEL) curriculum across the whole school builds SEL competence, allowing students to effectively apply knowledge, attitudes and skills necessary to understand and manage emotions, set and achieve positive goals, feel and show empathy for others, establish and maintain positive relationships and make responsible decisions (Weissberg 2015). Social-emotional competence is a multidimensional construct that is critical to success in school – especially for children at risk due to economic disadvantage, minority status and early emotional or behavioural problems. Adopting standards or other guidance for social, emotional and cognitive learning clarifies the kinds of competencies students need to be helped to develop and the kinds of practices that can help them accomplish these goals.

5. The school's physical environment (including facilities)

When students perceive their environment is in social disorder (e.g. through threatening, violent or disruptive interactions in school), they are less likely to feel safe or comfortable, to be able to learn, and less likely to optimise their potential and achievement in school (Tanner 2009). Therefore, the appearance of the school building and its classrooms matters. Removing evidence of physical disorder, such as broken windows, rubbish and graffiti, is critical – as is ensuring students' physical comfort (appropriate ambient noise and school temperature), order and organisation of the learning environment, surveillance around the school grounds, ratio of students to teachers and availability of resources.

Providing clean and inviting school buildings and grounds, including classrooms with natural light and views to the outside, enhances the school experience. Evidence also suggests that reducing the number of temporary buildings increases student attendance (Branham 2004). Displays of 'school pride', including student achievements and providing access to clear and comfortable indoor and outdoor walkways and spaces and other public spaces, foster a sense of community. More information about ways to enhance the school's physical environment is provided in Chapter 7.

6. The school's organisation and order

Where schools have clear and consistent policies or rules and order collaboratively developed with students and staff (and ideally families), this helps students, staff and families know what is expected of them and provides guidelines about individual and interpersonal conduct. It also sends a strong message to the whole school community about the school's values, expectations and actions to ensure a safe and supportive school environment and help build healthy, trusting relationships between school leaders and teachers.

The degree to which students, teachers and staff contribute to school decision-making also impacts expectations and practices as well as students' rule adherence and acceptance of consequences. This contribution to decision-making is best enabled through quality interpersonal relationships between and among students and school staff, including actions to support a positive school climate in school policies and mission statements to ensure a common vision among staff. It is also useful to establish whole-school guidelines for situations such as staff meeting agendas and for groups of staff (such as the wellbeing leadership team) dedicated to the implementation of programs and interventions.

While school climate is a critical consideration in all schools and across all grade levels, it is particularly important in large secondary school environments, which are typically more complex than primary schools. In secondary school, students have increasing need for autonomy, are spending more time with peers and are less dependent on adults (Way et al. 2007).

All schools need a dedicated school wellbeing team, with representation from the school community, to provide leadership, structure and organisation to the implementation of school wellbeing policies and practices. While all staff have a role in contributing to the wellbeing of students, their involvement requires leadership to provide a clear understanding of their role boundaries, especially staff with specialist roles, such as homeroom teachers, heads of year, heads of house or dean of students. These staff will also need access to knowledge and skills training to learn actions to support the school community's wellbeing and school policy and procedure guidelines, with sufficient supervision or support to ensure they are responding appropriately and working effectively.

7. The school's behavioural expectations and policy

The features of 'structure' (consistent and fair enforcement of school rules; equitable and fair treatment of students by teachers and staff) and 'support' (care and attention provided by adults) help to foster a positive school climate. Students are more likely to reject the values of the school if they do not believe in the legitimacy of the disciplinary actions or feel teachers are not fair or respectful of students (Stewart 2003).

Clearly defining, communicating and enforcing a fair and equitable system where rules outline acceptable and expected behaviour leads to a safer environment. Replacing zero-tolerance policies of school discipline with behavioural expectation policies focused on explicit teaching of social–emotional strategies, identification and promotion of prosocial behaviours and restorative discipline practices helps students learn key skills to develop responsibility for themselves and their community. Further, negotiating clear behavioural expectations and rules and engaging students in school decision-making is a critical part of 'authoritative' school discipline, which is a combination of structure and support in school (i.e. consistent rules, fairness and respect) (Gregory and Cornell 2009).

Focusing on relationships, especially with the use of restorative practices, helps to build a climate of healing the harm to relationships from wrongdoing or conflict (Cavanagh et al. 2007). For example, implementing effective and positive classroom management strategies that minimise the degree of competition and social comparison between students and provide greater support for students with behavioural challenges is essential. Small group sessions (i.e. no more than 4 students) facilitated by student support staff or external providers; or brief, regular individual student–staff contact meetings with students with behavioural issues are useful to discuss behavioural expectations or just to check in with students.

Information describing these behavioural expectations policies needs to be distributed, promoted and highly accessible to staff, students and families through a range of channels, such as through the school portal, intranet, student diaries, parent handbooks and staff induction and professional learning, to ensure these are understood, implemented fairly and consistently enforced.

Engagement of families

Much evidence shows that, while the home environment is a major contributing factor to students' wellbeing, school staff also can and do make an important difference over and above the contribution of the home environment (Runions et al. 2014). For example, research found that wellbeing practices that involved families were more likely to improve the school climate, than those where families were not involved (Mertens et al. 2020). Hence, it is critical for the wellbeing leadership team to ensure opportunities are provided to develop respectful, positive and meaningful partnerships with students' families.

Family engagement strategies need to include regularly sending information home to parents that is specific to their children, such as what social and emotional wellbeing skills they learned in class and involving parents in home-related activities. In addition to engaging with families about their own children's wellbeing, it is also important to share the school's wellbeing strategy and progress with the whole school community early and often (i.e. not as an afterthought). This can include a standing item at staff, parent and carer meetings; presentations of major wellbeing findings; key parent and carer representation on the wellbeing leadership team; and involving the community, as appropriate, in school wellbeing recommendations. These regular communication activities help to snowball the relevancy of the school's wellbeing effort to families.

Whole-school wellbeing practices that work inclusively with families are more effective. Sheridan et al. (2012) found that when teachers and families work together to support students, positive outcomes result, including for students experiencing difficulties. Some families, however, may not have time to participate in school activities or may feel hesitant to engage, or worse, not feel welcome or culturally safe in the school. Well-tailored messaging co-developed with diverse groups of parents can enable respectful family engagement that is proactive, culturally safe and relevant.

When wellbeing learnings at school are reinforced at home, this not only increases the impact of that information on student behaviour, but also increases the likelihood that families will support teacher implementation of wellbeing-related action. Examples of family engagement actions that may reinforce school wellbeing implementation efforts include:

> staff communicating regularly and proactively with all families about the positive wellbeing outcomes experienced by their child, such as progress when a student is experiencing difficulties, or small successes, such as effort to engage with students they don't know

> ensuring families have a clear, single point of first contact with the school – ideally, a homeroom teacher (whose job description ensures they know every student in their homeroom group very well) who is responsive and positive about family contact

- providing flexible arrangements and welcoming strategies to enhance families' engagement with and participation in wellbeing activities offered by the school
- providing culturally inclusive communication and activities for families from diverse cultural and ethnic backgrounds
- understanding family needs and interests and organising family and community wellbeing forums addressing issues relevant to their children
- providing a welcoming atmosphere for parents and visitors to the school with actions that encourage their participation in school initiatives and activities.

Lastly, the wellbeing leadership team needs to consider mechanisms that help to strengthen school staff and families' contact with allied health and social services and other partnerships to support student wellbeing in the wider community, such as with the local community sports, recreation or arts centres.

Chapter summary

There is robust evidence describing the many benefits for the whole school community of school leaders establishing, embedding and sustaining a positive school climate. Not only is school climate positively related to student academic achievement (including mitigating the negative effects of economic disadvantage on achievement), it also has a profound impact on students' mental and physical health, including helping students who are experiencing mental health difficulties. It is associated with or promotes safety, healthy relationships, reduced drug use, violence and other risk behaviours, motivated and engaged learning and teaching, teacher retention and school improvement efforts. And most importantly, the proactive and intentional leadership style of the principal largely predicts the quality of their school's climate.

This chapter describes high-impact actions that can be led by principals to improve the 7 key components of a positive school climate.

These are teacher–student and student–student relationships in a culture of equity and fairness; the school community's perception of the social, emotional and physical safety of the school; students' level of school connectedness, engagement and participation; the school's academic care and focus on social and emotional learning; the school's physical environment; the school's organisation and order; and the school's behavioural expectations and policy.

From the discussion so far, it is clear that school climate can be enhanced as part of school improvement processes and that school improvement processes are themselves influenced by the quality of the school climate. Hence on all levels, a strong focus on school climate by school leaders is critical.

The following table provides a checklist of high-impact actions school leaders can consider when reviewing and implementing policies and practices to improve school climate.

To improve our school climate we:	Not in place	Working towards	In place	Progressing well
Ensure the wellbeing leadership team has school community representation (including student and school leader participation) and meets regularly to drive the implementation of policies and practices to enhance school climate.				
Positively define a comprehensive school-wide vision for the school's climate (collaboratively with students, families and staff).				
Collect and curate school-level data from staff and students to benchmark, monitor and target practices and evaluate the effectiveness of the school climate.				
Use meaningful school-level data collected from staff and students, to operationalise improvement goals to enhance school climate.				
Use school-level data to determine which of the 7 school climate components are functioning well and contributing to the school's climate and what evidence-based policies and practices need to be implemented.				

Assess staff engagement and readiness and enable their involvement by sharing information, encouraging feedback and providing training and coaching support where needed, so staff can implement the selected policies and practices.				
Implement and monitor evidence-based school climate–related policies and practices that are adaptable, developmentally, contextually and culturally appropriate and meet school priorities.				
Regularly monitor and share implementation and student outcome data about the school climate with staff and refine implementation supports based on findings.				

References

Aldridge J, Ala'l K (2013) 'Assessing students' views of school climate: developing and validating the What's Happening In This School? (WHITS) questionnaire', *Improving Schools*, 16(1):47–66.

Aldridge JM, McChesney K (2018) 'The relationships between school climate and adolescent mental health and wellbeing: a systematic literature review', *International Journal of Educational Research*, 88:121–145.

Bartanen B, Grissom JA, Rogers LK (2019) 'The impacts of principal turnover', *Educational Evaluation and Policy Analysis*, 41(3):350–374.

Berkowitz R, Moore H, Astor RA, Benbenishty R (2017) 'A research synthesis of the associations between socioeconomic background, inequality, school climate, and academic achievement', *Review of Educational Research*, 87(2):425–469.

Bradshaw CP, Waasdorp TE, Debnam KJ, Johnson SL (2014) 'Measuring school climate in high schools: a focus on safety, engagement, and the environment', *Journal of School Health*, 84(9):593–604.

Branham D (2004) 'The wise man builds his house upon the rock: the effects of inadequate school building infrastructure on student attendance', *Social Science Quarterly*, 85(5):1112–1128.

Cavanagh T, Boyd S, Ridley K, Anthony G, Walshaw M, Hunter P, Rutherford J (2007) 'Focusing on relationships creates safety in schools', *Set: Research Information for Teachers*, 1:31–35.

Coelli M, Green DA (2012) 'Leadership effects: school principals and student outcomes, *Economics of Education Review*, 31(1):92–109.

Cohen J, McCabe L, Michelli NM, Pickeral T (2009) 'School climate: research, policy, practice, and teacher education', *Teachers College Record*, 111(1):180–213.

Cross D, Lester L, Barnes A, Cardoso P, Hadwen K (2015) 'If it's about me, why do it without me? Genuine student engagement in school cyberbullying education', *International Journal of Emotional Education*, 7(1):35–51.

Day C, Gu Q, Sammons P (2016) 'The impact of leadership on student outcomes: how successful school leaders use transformational and instructional strategies to make a difference', *Educational Administration Quarterly*, 52(2):221–258.

Deal TE, Peterson KD (1999) 'Shaping school culture: the heart of leadership', *Adolescence*, 34(136):802.

Deal TE, Peterson KD (2010) *Shaping school culture: pitfalls, paradoxes, and promises*, John Wiley & Sons, San Francisco, CA.

Durlak JA, Weissberg RP, Dymnicki AB, Taylor RD, Schellinger KB (2011) 'The impact of enhancing students' social and emotional learning: a meta-analysis of school-based universal interventions', *Child Development*, 82(1):405–432.

Gregory A, Cornell D (2009) '"Tolerating" adolescent needs: Moving beyond zero tolerance policies in high school', *Theory Into Practice*, 48(2):106–113.

Grissom JA, Bartanen B, Mitani H (2019) 'Principal sorting and the distribution of principal quality', *AERA Open*, 5(2):2332858419850094.

Grissom JA, Kalogrides D, Loeb S (2015) 'Using student test scores to measure principal performance', *Educational Evaluation and Policy Analysis*, 37(1):3–28.

Hall W (2017) 'The effectiveness of policy interventions for school bullying: a systematic review', *Journal of the Society for Social Work and Research*, 8(1):45–69.

Hoy WK, Hannum JW (1997) 'Middle school climate: An empirical assessment of organizational health and student achievement', *Educational Administration Quarterly*, 33(3):290–311.

Jones A, Shindler J (2016) 'Exploring the school climate–student achievement connection: making sense of why the first precedes the second', *Educational Leadership and Administration: Teaching and Program Development*, 27:35–51.

Kasen S, Cohen P, Chen H, Johnson JG, Crawford TN (2009) 'School climate and continuity of adolescent personality disorder symptoms', *Journal of Child Psychology and Psychiatry*, 50(12):1504–1512.

Klein J, Cornell D, Konold T (2012) 'Relationships between bullying, school climate, and student risk behaviors', *School Psychology Quarterly*, 27(3):154.

Klusmann U, Richter D, Lüdtke O (2016) 'Teachers' emotional exhaustion is negatively related to student achievement: evidence from a large-scale assessment study', *Journal of Educational Psychology*, 108:1193–1203.

Konishi C, Hymel S, Wong TKY, Waterhouse T (2021) 'School climate and bystander responses to bullying', *Psychology in the Schools*.

Kuperminc GP, Leadbeater BJ, Emmons C, Blatt SJ (1997) 'Perceived school climate and difficulties in the social adjustment of middle school students', *Applied Developmental Science*, 1(2):76–88.

Kutsyuruba B, Klinger DA, Hussain A (2015) 'Relationships among school climate, school safety, and student achievement and well-being: a review of the literature', *Review of Education*, 3(2):103–35.

Mertens E, Deković M, Leijten P, Van Londen M, Reitz E (2020) 'Components of schoolbased interventions stimulating students' intrapersonal and interpersonal domains: a meta-analysis', *Clinical Child and Family Psychology Review*, 23:605–631.

Mitra DL (2004) 'The significance of students: can increasing "student voice" in schools lead to gains in youth development?', *Teachers College Record*, 106(4):651–688.

Okonofua JA, Eberhardt JL (2015) 'Two strikes: race and the disciplining of young students', *Psychological Science*, 26(5):617–624.

Riley P (2013) *The Australian principal occupational health, safety & well-being survey: 2013 data*, Australian Catholic University, Melbourne.

Runions KC, Vitaro F, Cross D, Boivin M (2014) 'Teacher–child relationship, parenting, and growth in likelihood and severity of physical aggression in the early school years', *Merrill-Palmer Quarterly*, 60(3):274–301.

Rutledge SA, Cohen-Vogel L, Osborne-Lampkin LT, Roberts RL (2015) 'Understanding effective high schools: evidence for personalization for academic and social emotional learning', *American Educational Research Journal*, 52(6):1060–1092.

Sheridan SM, Witte AL, Holmes SR, Coutts MJ, Dent AL, Kunz GM, Wu C (2012) 'A randomized trial examining the effects of conjoint behavioral consultation and the mediating role of the parent–teacher relationship', *School Psychology Review*, 41(1):23–46.

Stewart EA (2003) 'School social bonds, school climate, and school misbehavior: a multilevel analysis', *Justice Quarterly*, 20(3):575–604.

Tanner CK (2009) 'Effects of school design on student outcomes', *Journal of Educational Administration*, 47(3):381–399.

Thapa A, Cohen J, Guffey S, Higgins-D'Alessandro A (2013) 'A review of school climate research', *Review of Educational Research*, 83(3):357–385.

Tichnor-Wagner A, Allen D (2016) 'Accountable for care: cultivating caring school communities in urban high schools', *Leadership and Policy in Schools*, 15(4):406–447.

Voight A (2015) 'Student voice for school-climate improvement: a case study of an urban middle school', *Journal of Community & Applied Social Psychology*, 25(4):310–326.

Wang C, Berry B, Swearer SM (2013) 'The critical role of school climate in effective bullying prevention', *Theory Into Practice*, 52(4):296–302.

Wang MT, Degol JL, Amemiya J, Parr A, Guo J (2020) 'Classroom climate and children's academic and psychological wellbeing: a systematic review and meta-analysis', *Developmental Review*, 57:100912.

Way N, Reddy R, Rhodes J (2007) 'Students' perceptions of school climate during the middle school years: associations with trajectories of psychological and behavioral adjustment', *American Journal of Community Psychology*, 40(3):194–213.

Weissberg RP, Durlak JA, Domitrovich CE, Gullotta TP (2015) 'Social and emotional learning: past, present, and future' in Durlak JA, Domitrovich CE, Weissberg RP, Gullotta TP (eds) *Handbook of social and emotional learning: research and practice*, The Guilford Press.

Zullig KJ, Collins R, Ghani N, Patton JM, Scott Huebner E, Ajamie J (2014) 'Psychometric support of the school climate measure in a large, diverse sample of adolescents: a replication and extension', *Journal of School Health*, 84(2):82–90.

Zullig KJ, Matthews-Ewald MR (2014) 'School climate: definition, measurement, and application', in Furlong MJ, Gilman R, Huebner ES (eds) *Handbook of positive psychology in schools*, Routledge/Taylor & Francis Group.

CHAPTER 4

Teacher relationships and classroom practices to build student wellbeing

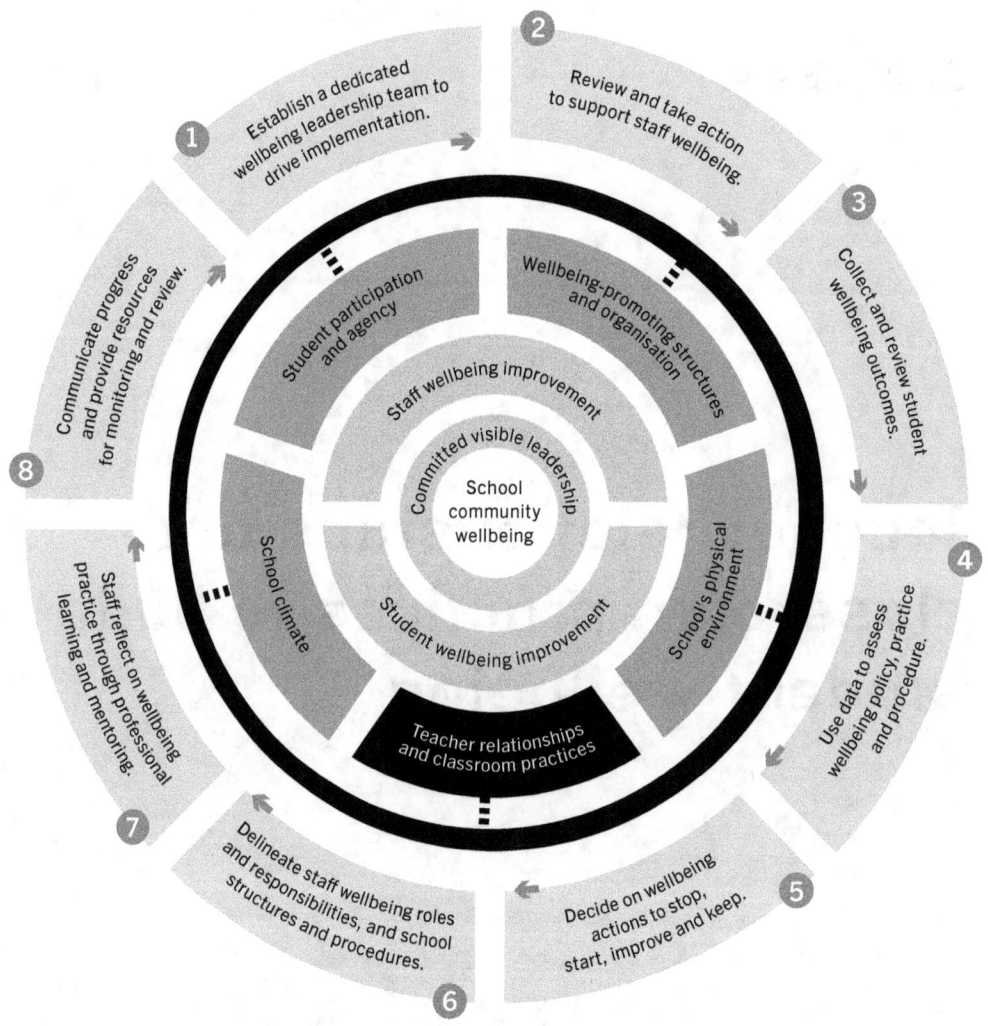

Figure 4.1. Teacher relationships and classroom practices

While the synergistic link between students' wellbeing and their academic outcomes is almost irrefutable, proactive school-based actions to improve student wellbeing are often not embedded nor institutionalised in policy and practice. Consequently, wellbeing policies and practices are often not systematically addressed, or included as key performance indicators for school staff. This chapter argues that just 'responding to students' wellbeing needs' is different from embedding actions to promote, protect and support student wellbeing within the fabric of a school, where it is a driving purpose.

This chapter discusses how school leaders can focus the collective responsibility of all staff, particularly teaching staff, on providing universal, proactive and targeted actions, to support students' wellbeing. It describes high-impact practices school leaders can use to encourage and enable teachers to enhance their own classroom climates through their relationships with their students, their academic care (teaching style), their learning environment organisation, and management and explicit teaching of social and emotional learning curriculum. Interestingly, Holfve-Sabel (2014) found significant differences in student wellbeing at a group level between same-grade classrooms in the same school, suggesting that the classroom climate, that is, the pedagogy, organisation and personality of the teacher and the socialisation of the group of students, can impact student wellbeing over and above school climate and the influence of the school leader.

Many approaches can be used to build a positive classroom climate, ranging from implicit whole-class activities (such as creating a warm, safe and orderly classroom environment) to explicit whole-class activities (social and emotional skills taught via curriculum). Both implicit and explicit approaches are discussed in this chapter.

School leaders may consider encouraging their wellbeing team to map the implicit and explicit social and emotional learning policy and practices offered by the school to better understand the actions being taken, with which students and when, to address student wellbeing outcomes as outlined in Chapter 2.

Implicit actions teaching staff can take to improve student wellbeing

Creating a positive classroom climate

A positive classroom climate is achieved through the quality of teacher relationships with each student, the way teaching staff organise their learning environments and the quality of their pedagogy. Classroom climate (as distinct from the school climate – see Chapter 3) comprises the social, emotional and physical features of the learning environments, created by teaching staff for their students, to enhance teacher–student interactions (e.g. teacher–student relationships, learning environment organisation, order and rule clarity and teaching quality). Classroom climate is one of the most important influences on how students learn, behave and develop socially and emotionally (Wang, Hofkens et al. 2020; Wang, L. Degol et al. 2020).

While classroom climate is the primary responsibility of teaching staff, it is also impacted by the quality of school leadership and the school's policies and procedures. For example, when students feel safe at school, they are more able to respond well to the learning environment and form positive relationships with their teachers (Crosnoe et al. 2004).

It is a critical role of school leaders to establish policies and procedures that enable all students to consistently experience a positive classroom climate through the practices of each teacher. This in turn reinforces the school's climate. For example, school leaders need to ensure policies and staff key performance indicators (KPIs) require staff to build positive relationships and interactions with **all** the students in their classroom(s). At a minimum, this means knowing every student's name and at least one strength and something unique about each of them so teachers can connect with students or invite their expertise in the classroom. This knowledge shows students they are valued and important and helps to ensure that every student feels connected to at least one adult in the school. Every positive interaction with students counts towards improving their wellbeing and the quality of their learning.

Leading a school climate that drives positive student–teacher and peer relationships, effective teaching (including the implementation of social and emotional learning) and productive learning environment management and organisation is key to building a positive classroom climate. However, school staff may require professional development to ensure they have the knowledge and skills to build a deep conceptual understanding of wellbeing and to ensure they are confident using the approaches necessary to nurture student wellbeing. This knowledge is linked to increased student competence and autonomy, greater engagement in learning, more prosocial skills and fewer behavioural issues (Wang, L. Degol et al. 2020).

Pianta and Hamre (2009a) suggest the structure and nature of teacher–student interactions in a positive classroom climate include 3 dimensions:

1. Social and emotional support
2. Instructional support
3. Learning environment organisation and management.

Teaching staff can take the following classroom climate-building actions that align with these dimensions:

> Positive social and emotional support

Roorda et al. (2011) recommend learning environment features that support students' social and emotional wellbeing, such as:

- creating a classroom climate where students feel safe
- ensuring positive student–teacher relationships (i.e. where teachers are friendly adult role models, but not students' friends)
- ensuring positive student–student relationships
- building connectedness, trust and mutual respect
- being responsive to students' social and emotional strengths, interests and needs.

When these student–teacher and student–student relationships are strong, there is also less misbehaviour, especially in secondary schools (Wang et al. 2013). Swan (2021) found that caring and empathetic teaching staff 'know and connect with students, are in tune with what students think and feel; use collaboration and operate as a team and display high levels of social and emotional support and model "I have empathy"'. These staff model key social and emotional messages like 'I am interested in you'; 'I am a safe person to be around'; 'I am consistent'; 'I understand how you may be feeling'; 'I can be a helper'; and 'I will be supportive'.

> **Instructional support** through a pedagogy of academic caring.

Academic care includes actions teaching staff take that connect to and engage with students in the learning environment to improve their cognitive development. These actions align with each student's strengths and support their individual needs while promoting relevant and meaningful participation. Teachers demonstrate high academic expectations; connect prior and new knowledge; and provide challenging tasks and quality feedback. Academic care actions also include learning and using student names, encouraging and praising student effort, checking in with students, noticing little things, focusing on continuous personal improvement and promoting effort versus competition for academic scores (Addison 2017).

> **Learning environment organisation and management** are the positive actions and learning environment routines teaching staff establish to provide safety, create consistent expectations, reduce classroom chaos and help students remain engaged in their learning.

These routines support students to stay on task, to persist with learning challenges and to develop academic and social and emotional skills. This includes enabling well-functioning, productive learning environments, by providing explicit expectations about behaviour; consistently reinforcing learning environment rules while recognising and rewarding student attempts to comply; and providing behaviour supports to prevent, or fairly and effectively manage, poor behaviour (Catalano et al. 2003).

Flexible learning spaces are an example of how learning environments can be organised to increase student autonomy (self-directed learning) and relatedness (through authentic teacher-student and student-student collaboration) and thereby promote social and emotional wellbeing (Kariippanon et al. 2018). Creating calm and positive learning environments allows students to focus on learning and development in the absence of conflict and distraction.

Evidence suggests that all the above 3 dimensions of building a classroom climate, when implemented well, are important for students' academic achievement, although these were found to be more powerful in primary compared to secondary schools (Allen et al. 2013). In a positive classroom climate, students can build stronger relationships with teaching staff and other students and are better able to regulate their learning and behaviour (Addison 2012).

School leaders need to encourage staff to reflect on their own classroom practices, including their relationships with all students, their teaching style, learning environment organisation and management and how well they link the utility of their content to students' lives. Importantly, supportive teacher–student relationships, other positive interactions with the school community and providing a positive learning environment that builds a sense of belonging are critical protective factors for students who experience socioeconomic disadvantage and face more personal adversity, such as trauma (Smith et al. 2017).

As will be discussed in Chapter 5, students' learning, health and develop-ment are also enhanced when they perceive their learning environment helps them to build autonomy, belonging and competence (Connell and Wellborn 1991). This means students have opportunities to:

> make choices and determine their own behaviour ('autonomy')

> develop positive relationships in an emotionally supportive environment with their teachers and other students ('belonging')

> build 'competence' when the learning environment is well organised and structured and by knowing what they need to do to be successful (Skinner et al. 2009).

Positive classroom climate for First Nations students

To effectively support First Nations students in their learning and to provide a culturally secure, positive school experience, Harslett et al. (2000) recommend teachers:

> include cultural relevance and recognition in the curriculum and classroom environment

> understand First Nations students are often more independent than other students

> manage student behaviour through positive reinforcement, subtlety, consistency and fairness

> don't chastise or embarrass students in front of others and remain flexible and non-confrontational

> set challenging and achievable objectives

> be patient, persistent and good listeners

> work with students in a relationship rather than in authoritarian mode

> engage students in learning with a good blend of verbal and written work

> encourage discussion, limit writing and demonstrate with visual modelling.

Teaching staff who work with First Nations students must have an understanding of 'Aboriginal culture, history, and students' kinship and home backgrounds; an ability to develop good relationships with Aboriginal students and their families, a sense of humour, and preparedness to invest time to interact with Aboriginal students out of the classroom in order to strengthen relationships' (Harslett et al. 2000:37). Ideally, provided they are consulted and in agreement, First Nations staff in the school could provide regular professional learning for all staff, to enhance these understandings and skills. Many of these characteristics are critical to help support students from any non-dominant cultural group.

Building teacher-student relationships throughout the learning journey

The salience of quality teacher–student relationships in promoting each student's wellbeing can't be over-emphasised. Student wellbeing is about people, not programs. Positive teacher–student relationships are associated with higher student general executive function, memory and inhibition (Vandenbroucke et al. 2018), increased student engagement and academic achievement (Roorda et al. 2011) and fewer behaviour and conduct problems (Marzano and Marzano 2003; Wang et al. 2013; Wang et al. 2010).

The evidence is strong – when students like their teachers, they learn better. Students' sense of safety, trust, mutual respect and the warmth that comes from these positive relationships build students' connectedness to the school environment and give them confidence to explore new ideas and take risks that are essential to learning (Murray and Greenberg 2000).

Bonds between teaching staff and individual students and the level of 'care' perceived by students as being provided by teaching staff influences multiple levels of students' school experiences (Roorda et al. 2011). Students who feel noticed and valued are more likely to work harder and to care about themselves and others; those who feel their teachers are supportive have higher levels of self-efficacy and are more likely to persevere with complex tasks (Loukas and Robinson 2004); and those who think their teachers care about them and are supportive and approachable are more likely to seek help when needed, achieve better and have fewer antisocial behaviours (Wang et al. 2010).

While meaningful, reciprocated relationships between teaching staff and students, where students feel genuinely listened to, are important to students at all ages, this is especially true in the early school years, as these experiences can shape students' future relationships with teaching staff and other students and with formal education overall. Research has found that the quality of teacher–student relationships in the first year of school is associated with more student on-task behaviour (Pianta and Hamre 2009b), later academic success and positive behavioural outcomes for students (Hamre and Pianta 2001).

In later primary years, positive teacher–student relationships have been associated with greater student engagement and higher maths and reading scores in disadvantaged students (Rimm-Kaufman et al. 2015; Elias and Haynes 2008). When upper primary students and secondary students feel well supported by their teachers, they also report fewer social and emotional difficulties, including fewer symptoms of depression (Arbeau et al. 2010; Reddy et al. 2003; Wang et al. 2013); they are also more likely to engage in prosocial behaviour (Davidson et al. 2010; Wang et al. 2013).

In secondary school, social support and respect from teachers is related to higher levels of student motivation and engagement (Greene et al. 2004), better behaviour and stronger academic grades (Wang and Eccles 2012). Resnick et al. (1997) note that student connectedness to teaching staff and the school is also associated with higher social and emotional wellbeing and lower levels of violence and risky behaviours. Students in learning environments where their teachers use empathetic caring pedagogy are more likely to report their teacher provides emotional support, their classroom feels more like a family and their contributions are valued in class (Maloney and Matthews 2020).

Relationships with school staff are also important when students are experiencing difficulties, including when student behaviour doesn't meet school standards. If staff have invested deeply in getting to know their students, they will have 'banked credit' with these students from which they can 'draw down' in times of need. This credit is important, given many students don't typically seek the help of school staff when they are experiencing difficulties, especially boys.

Leadership practice idea: case study

One school whose mantra is 'to know every student' led an exercise with their staff to understand how much they really know about all their students. Taking one year level per staff meeting, they placed the photographs of the faces of these students on the walls around the staff room. They then asked staff to write something positive they knew about each student (even details like 'they play basketball at lunchtime') on the paper beneath each name. Staff were then asked to reflect on what was written – firstly, to read and learn something they perhaps didn't know about each student and secondly, to notice for which students little was written. These photographs and notes were removed following the meeting and the positive information about each student was recorded and distributed to staff through the wellbeing leaders (in this school, the heads of house) for their reference. Staff were asked to try to actively learn more about all students, but particularly about those for whom little was written. This exercise was carried out for each year group in the first half of the year and then repeated in the second half to see if more was known about each student.

Encouraging peers to be proactive carers too

Given caring about student wellbeing is also the right and responsibility of each student – not school staff alone – it is important that school leaders embed an ethos, policies and practices that encourage and enable students to proactively support the wellbeing of their peers, other students, their teachers and their family.

Positive classroom climate and student social and emotional wellbeing is enhanced not only by teacher–student relationships, but also when students interact positively with each other. For both primary and secondary students, teacher practices need to provide opportunities for prosocial and cooperative work, to build high-quality positive relationships between students and ideally across year groups. These practices also help to increase student connectedness and engagement to school (Solomon et al. 1996) and their social and emotional development (Hoglund and Leadbeater 2004).

Research has found that peer wellbeing predicts individual student wellbeing (King and Datu 2017). However, for students (and staff) to be able to support others' wellbeing, they need to understand the spectrum of care and appropriate responses they can reasonably provide. This spectrum includes actions to promote and protect their own and others' wellbeing, and actions to prevent or reduce harm, such as mental and physical 'first aid' (i.e. providing help to someone until they can receive appropriate professional treatment, or until the situation is resolved). Mental health first aid needs to be as fundamental and as comprehensively taught in schools to support wellbeing as is physical first aid.

Explicit actions teaching staff can take to improve student wellbeing

As teaching staff and the learning environments they create have a central role in the development of student wellbeing, there is a need for school leaders to provide clarity regarding teaching staff role expectations.

School leaders need to ensure teaching staff know how their actions, their relationships with students and the learning environments they create, can enhance or harm the wellbeing of students and the development of protective factors (i.e. factors that can reduce the negative impact of issues like mental health problems, such as connectedness to family and friends) (Konu et al. 2002; Nadge 2005). The following section addresses explicit actions teaching staff can take through the teaching of social and emotional skills to improve student wellbeing and to prevent poor wellbeing outcomes.

Teaching social and emotional skills to all students

Strong evidence shows that embedding the explicit teaching of social and emotional (non-cognitive) skills for all year groups, using quality evidence-based curriculum and pedagogy, is necessary to improve the health, wellbeing and achievement of students and that these impacts persist overtime.

Students' social and emotional learning is linked by research conducted by Wigelsworth et al. (2022) to:

> improved social and emotional skills
> lower levels of mental health difficulties, such as anxiety and depression
> higher life satisfaction and connectedness to school
> better academic performance
> improved resilience and positive affect
> improved relationships with peers
> fewer behaviour problems.

This list can be built on by Gaffney et al. (2021) who suggest student social and emotional learning is also linked to:

> fewer problems with bullying, violence and alcohol and other drug use.

Importantly, the benefits of developing students' social and emotional skills appear to extend to the school climate and to teaching staff, with teachers reporting lower stress levels, higher job satisfaction and better behaviour from and relationships with students (Jennings and Greenberg 2009).

Like all skills-based learning, such as reading and numeracy, the earlier social and emotional skills are taught well, integrated, embedded across learning areas, modelled by teachers, and practised, the better the outcome for students. Research, for example, found children's social skills measured in the first year of school predicted outcomes 20 years later, including educational attainment, employment, crime, substance use and mental health (Jones et al. 2015). Social and emotional skills need dedicated time and to be taught formally and informally with a range of strategies, to enable students to practise these skills in context.

School leaders need to reinforce school-wide behavioural expectations and norms related to social and emotional learning via whole-school activities, by aligning the ethos and behaviour policies with the learning of social and emotional skills. Further, to optimise and monitor the implementation of social and emotional learning across the school, leaders need to prioritise training for all staff, establishing a shared vision and involving the school community (especially students).

Robust research also found that social and emotional learning (SEL) has a direct impact on student academic outcomes. A meta-analysis of 213 school-based SEL interventions involving 270,034 K–12 students led by Durlak et al. (2011) found, compared to controls, that students showed significantly improved social and emotional skills, attitudes and behaviour, and that students' academic achievement improved by an average of 11 percentile points. While a 2020 systematic review of school student wellbeing programs (Dix et al. 2020) found that the programs had an overall impact on social–emotional, behavioural and cognitive outcomes; those programs that explicitly addressed SEL were found to be the most effective for promoting student wellbeing and literacy outcomes. Interestingly, the non-cognitive skills of emotional intelligence and conscientiousness were found in a meta-analysis by MacCann et al. (2020) to be the second most important, robust and significant predictors of academic achievement, after a student's intelligence.

Providing social and emotional learning experiences that are effective

The review of SEL programs by Dix et al. (2020) found that the most effective programs were delivered by trained teaching staff; involved the whole school community (versus only targeting specific students); were delivered to students in groups of 11 to 20 (compared to one-on-one or large groups) and included age- and culturally appropriate content.

Identifying effective social and emotional learning resources can, however, be challenging, given the plethora of 'wellbeing' resources marketed to schools, most of which have limited or no evidence of their effectiveness in Australian schools and are largely 'one-size-fits-all' resources, not designed to meet the unique context of each school or the strengths and needs of each school's students.

The most prominent national wellbeing resources are the *Australian Student Wellbeing Framework* (ESA 2018), the Australian Curriculum, Assessment and Reporting Authority's (ACARA 2023) *Personal and Social Capability (Version 8.4)* and *Be You* (Be You 2023a).

The Be You initiative provides a mental health and wellbeing *Programs Directory* (Be You 2023b) that rates over 70 wellbeing programs available to Australian schools. The Australian *Friendly Schools* (2023) SEL resources and training is one of only a few programs to receive Be You's highest rating. The Friendly Schools resources, comprehensively developed and tested over a 20-year period in Western Australia, provides a whole-school intervention for student social and emotional skill development (Cross et al. 2018). The Friendly Schools resources have significant peer-reviewed evidence demonstrating their effectiveness in improving the social and emotional wellbeing of primary and secondary students (Cross et al. 2011; Cross et al. 2018; Cross et al. 2019). Via robust, validated and reliable survey measures, students self-reported reduced stress, loneliness and depressive symptoms, as well as improved perceptions of school safety and less bullying perpetration and victimisation (Cross et al. 2018).

Some Australian schools use resources developed by the Collaborative for Academic, Social and Emotional Learning (CASEL) to support their SEL teaching. CASEL (2020) describes the 5 key SEL competencies that students need to explicitly develop as self-awareness, self-management, social awareness, relationship skills and responsible decision-making. These categorisations of SEL are very similar to ACARA's (2023) *Personal and Social Capability*, which combines the CASEL 'decision-making' and 'relationship skills' competencies into one category called 'social management'.

Quality training and provision of other implementation supports are often needed to build the skills of teaching staff to deliver SEL programs. The *Australian Student Wellbeing Framework* (ESA 2018) and CASEL (2023) provide some self-assessment, reflection, planning and training tools for teaching staff to review their practices and pedagogy to determine how well they promote their students' wellbeing. The Australian *Student Wellbeing Hub* also includes online professional learning modules for educators (ESA 2020).

Non-traditional teaching practices that promote student wellbeing

Wellbeing hubs in school

Purpose-built wellbeing hubs are becoming more prevalent in schools, ideally co-designed with students and staff to provide specific services to promote and support the school community's wellbeing.

In a review of the evidence regarding the use of school libraries to support student wellbeing, Merga (2020) found that libraries can effectively support students in 3 ways by:

> operating as safe spaces for students

> promoting and resourcing mental health and wellbeing initiatives

> supporting and promoting reading for pleasure.

Some schools use libraries or other lunchtime locations with higher teacher-to-student ratios to provide support to students who may be feeling lonely or having difficulty making friends. Turning off computers during lunch breaks and providing more 'face-to-face' activities, such as board games in the library, and through 'clubs' may also help to encourage lonely students to play and get to know each other.

Animal-assisted social and emotional learning

The presence of animals, such as dogs, cats, horses and birds, in school settings to support student wellbeing is becoming an increasingly common practice. Animals can provide students with comfort, calm or safety and can help to direct students' attention in positive ways. A therapy dog or comfort dog, for example, is used by some schools to provide additional attention and emotional support to students. There is encouraging evidence of the potential benefits of including animals in educational practice and evidence of improved emotional wellbeing among students with behavioural issues (Brelsford et al. 2017). An equine therapy program offered to Aboriginal school students in the Kimberly region of Western Australia has shown positive results for those participating (Emerging Minds, 29 April 2022).

Outdoor play and movement breaks

Breaking up class time with short physical activity breaks has been shown to improve students' concentration, cognition, learning outcomes and behaviour and to promote student wellbeing (Becker et al. 2017). These breaks are typically 5 to 15 minutes long and are most effective when scheduled each day around learning environment transitions, helping students reset themselves for optimal learning. The movement breaks are best used to bring student energy up or down. A large study of 5,463 students across 332 schools examined the impact of 3 different 15-minute outdoor activities on student cognition and wellbeing (Booth et al. 2020). These self-paced outdoor activities were associated with improved cognition and wellbeing scores. Some 5-minute wellbeing breaks are available on the *Wellbeing Fives* (ReachOut 2022) page of the ReachOut website (a wellbeing support initiative for young people).

Project-based learning

Project-based learning is an increasingly popular pedagogic framework to promote deeper and more active learning through authentic student engagement and application of learning to issues relevant to students. Allison et al. (2015) empirically investigated the impact of project-based learning on secondary students' health and wellbeing. These students reported increased skills to cope with challenges, build relationships and take responsibility – personal capabilities that are important in contributing to health and wellbeing.

Chapter summary

This chapter shows that the importance of quality teacher relationships with students cannot be overstated. Students' relationships with teachers have a powerful influence on their experiences of and connection to school and on their wellbeing and academic outcomes. School leaders need to actively encourage, train and reward staff effort to use both formal and informal opportunities to build and sustain positive relationships with students to ensure they are well known and supported.

Research suggests that whole-school interventions, not just curriculum alone, are the most effective means to improve student social and emotional wellbeing. The classroom climate and academic care provided by teachers, as well as their pedagogy, are critical to establishing caring and safe learning environments, improved classroom management and teaching. This in turn enables students to feel valued, more motivated and engaged in their learning and to develop social and emotional skills that positively influence their wellbeing and academic achievement, especially among students experiencing difficulties.

Not all classroom curricula that aim to improve students' social and emotional skills are created equal. School leaders need to ensure their staff implement quality evidence-based resources (ideally tested in Australia via a randomised control trial) that are SAFE (sequenced, active, focused and explicit) and embed these deeply to meet their school context and the specific strengths and needs of their students.

The table below provides a checklist of high-impact learning environment actions school leaders can encourage and enable teaching staff to implement to build student wellbeing.

In our school, staff:	Not in place	Working towards	In place	Progressing well
Know the names and something unique about all the students they teach.				
Work to build positive and supportive relationships with all the students in their care.				
Use their pedagogy and relationships with students to create a warm, safe and orderly learning environment.				
Teach social and emotional skills explicitly.				
Use SEL curricula that are evidence based and SAFE (sequenced, active, focused and explicit).				
Integrate and role model SEL skills in everyday teaching across all learning areas to help all students to succeed.				

Use everyday formal and informal situations effectively to model, teach and give students opportunities to practise their social and emotional skills.				
Receive adequate professional learning in how to address social and emotional learning to teach their students, manage their classrooms and support students with challenging behaviour more effectively.				
Have common understandings and use a shared language of social and emotional learning.				
Use systems established to recognise and celebrate students' effective use of social and emotional skills.				

References

ACARA (Australian Curriculum, Assessment and Reporting Authority) (2023) *Personal and Social Capability (Version 8.4)*, ACARA website, accessed 26 January 2023. https://www.australiancurriculum.edu.au/f-10-curriculum/general-capabilities/personal-and-social-capability/

Addison B (2017) 'Looms and weavers: teaching and the creation of knowledge and wisdom', *Australian Educational Leader*, 39(2):45–46.

Addison BV (2012) 'Academic care, classroom pedagogy and the house group teacher: "making hope practical" in uncertain times', *Pastoral Care in Education*, 30(4):303–315.

Allen J, Gregory A, Mikami A, Lun J, Hamre B, Pianta R (2013) 'Observations of effective teacher–student interactions in secondary school classrooms: predicting student achievement with the Classroom Assessment Scoring System—Secondary', *School Psychology Review*, 42(1):76–98.

Allison P, Gray S, Sproule J, Nash C, Martindale R, Wang J (2015) 'Exploring contributions of project-based learning to health and wellbeing in secondary education, *Improving Schools*, 18(3):207–220.

Arbeau KA, Coplan RJ, Weeks M (2010) 'Shyness, teacher–child relationships, and socio-emotional adjustment in grade 1', *International Journal of Behavioral Development*, 34(3):259–269.

Be You (2023a) *Be You* [website], accessed 26 January 2023. https://beyou.edu.au/

Be You (2023b) *Programs Directory*, BeYou website, accessed 26 January 2023. https://beyou.edu.au/resources/programs-directory

Becker C, Lauterbach G, Spengler S, Dettweiler U, Mess F (2017) 'Effects of regular classes in outdoor education settings: a systematic review on students' learning, social and health dimensions', *International Journal of Environmental Research and Public Health*, 14(5):485.

Booth JN, Chesham RA, Brooks NE, Gorely T, Moran CN (2020) 'A citizen science study of short physical activity breaks at school: improvements in cognition and wellbeing with self-paced activity', *BMC Med*, 18,62.

Brelsford VL, Meints K, Gee NR, Pfeffer K (2017) 'Animal-assisted interventions in the classroom – a systematic review', *International Journal of Environmental Research and Public Health*, 14(7):669.

CASEL (Collaborative for Academic Social and Emotional Learning) (2020) *CASEL's SEL Framework*, CASEL website, accessed 26 January. https://casel.org/casel-sel-framework-11-2020/

CASEL (Collaborative for Academic Social and Emotional Learning) (2023) *Resources*, CASEL website, accessed 26 January. https://schoolguide.casel.org/resources/

Catalano RF, Mazza JJ, Harachi TW, Abbott RD, Haggerty KP, Fleming CB (2003) 'Raising healthy children through enhancing social development in elementary school: results after 1.5 years', *Journal of School Psychology*, 41(2):143–164.

Connell JP, Wellborn JG (1991) 'Competence, autonomy, and relatedness: a motivational analysis of self-system processes', in Gunnar MR, Sroufe LA (eds) *Self processes and development*, Lawrence Erlbaum Associates, Inc, Mahwah, NJ.

Crosnoe R, Johnson MK, Elder GH (2004) 'Intergenerational bonding in school: the behavioral and contextual correlates of student–teacher relationships', *Sociology of Education*, 77(1):60–81.

Cross D, Monks H, Hall M, Shaw T, Pintabona Y, Erceg E, Hamilton G, Roberts C, Waters S, Lester L (2011) 'Three-year results of the Friendly Schools whole-of-school intervention on children's bullying behaviour', *British Educational Research Journal*, 37(1):105–129.

Cross D, Runions KC, Shaw T, Wong JW, Campbell M, Pearce N, Burns S, Lester L, Barnes A, Resnicow K (2019) 'Friendly Schools universal bullying prevention intervention: effectiveness with secondary school students', *International Journal of Bullying Prevention*, 1(1):45–57.

Cross D, Shaw T, Epstein M, Pearce N, Barnes A, Burns S, Waters S, Lester L, Runions K (2018) 'Impact of the Friendly Schools whole-school intervention on transition to secondary school and adolescent bullying behaviour', *European Journal of Education*, 53(4):495–513.

Davidson AJ, Gest SD, Welsh JA (2010) 'Relatedness with teachers and peers during early adolescence: an integrated variable-oriented and person-oriented approach', *Journal of School Psychology*, 48(6):483–510.

Dix K, Ahmed SK, Carslake T, Sniedze-Gregory S, O'Grady E, Trevitt J (2020) *Student health and wellbeing: a systematic review of intervention research examining effective student wellbeing in schools and their academic outcomes*, Main report and executive summary, Evidence for Learning, Social Ventures, Australia.

Durlak JA, Weissberg RP, Dymnicki AB, Taylor RD, Schellinger KB (2011) 'The impact of enhancing students' social and emotional learning: a meta-analysis of school-based universal interventions', *Child Development*, 82(1):405–432.

Elias MJ, Haynes NM (2008) 'Social competence, social support, and academic achievement in minority, low-income, urban elementary school children', *School Psychology Quarterly*, 23(4):474.

Emerging Minds (29 April 2022) 'Equine therapy for Aboriginal and Torres Strait Islander children', Emerging Minds website, accessed 26 January 2023. https://emergingminds.com.au/resources/podcast/equine-therapy-for-aboriginal-and-torres-strait-islander-children/

ESA (Education Services Australia) (2018) *Australian Student Wellbeing Framework*, Education Council, Carlton South, VIC, accessed 17 January 2023. https://studentwellbeinghub.edu.au/educators/framework

ESA (Education Services Australia) (2020) *Professional learning courses*, Student Wellbeing Hub website, accessed 26 January 2023. https://studentwellbeinghub.edu.au/educators/professional-learning-courses

Friendly Schools (2023) *Friendly Schools* [website], accessed 26 January. https://friendlyschools.com.au/

Gaffney H, Ttofi MM, Farrington DP (2021) 'Effectiveness of school-based programs to reduce bullying perpetration and victimization: an updated systematic review and meta-analysis', *Campbell Systematic Reviews*, 17(2):e1143.

Greene BA, Miller RB, Crowson HM, Duke BL, Akey KL (2004) 'Predicting high school students' cognitive engagement and achievement: contributions of classroom perceptions and motivation', *Contemporary Educational Psychology*, 29(4):462–482.

Hamre BK, Pianta RC (2001) 'Early teacher–child relationships and the trajectory of children's school outcomes through eighth grade', *Child Development*, 72(2):625–638.

Harslett M, Harrison B, Godfrey J, Partington G, Richer K (2000) 'Teacher perceptions of the characteristics of effective teachers of Aboriginal middle school students', *Australian Journal of Teacher Education*, 25(2):37–45.

Hoglund WL, Leadbeater BJ (2004) 'The effects of family, school, and classroom ecologies on changes in children's social competence and emotional and behavioral problems in first grade', *Developmental Psychology*, 40(4):533.

Holfve-Sabel MA (2014) 'Learning, interaction and relationships as components of student well-being: differences between classes from student and teacher perspective', *Social Indicators Research*, 119(3):1535–1555.

Jennings PA, Greenberg MT (2009) 'The prosocial classroom: teacher social and emotional competence in relation to student and classroom outcomes', *Review of Educational Research*, 79(1):491–525.

Jones DE, Greenberg M, Crowley M (2015) 'Early social–emotional functioning and public health: the relationship between kindergarten social competence and future wellness', *American Journal of Public Health*, 105(11):2283–2290.

Kariippanon KE, Cliff DP, Lancaster SL, Okely AD, Parrish A-M (2018) 'Perceived interplay between flexible learning spaces and teaching, learning and student wellbeing', *Learning Environments Research*, 21(3):301–320.

King RB, Datu JA (2017) 'Happy classes make happy students: classmates' well-being predicts individual student well-being', *Journal of School Psychology*, 65:116–128.

Konu A, Alanen E, Lintonen T, Rimpelä M (2002) 'Factor structure of the school well-being model', *Health Education Research*, 17(6):732–742.

Loukas A, Robinson S (2004) 'Examining the moderating role of perceived school climate in early adolescent adjustment', *Journal of Research on Adolescence*, 14(2):209–233.

MacCann C, Jiang Y, Brown LER, Double KS, Bucich M, Minbashian A (2020) 'Emotional intelligence predicts academic performance: a meta-analysis', *Psychological Bulletin*, 146(2):150–186.

Maloney T, Matthews JS (2020) 'Teacher care and students' sense of connectedness in the urban mathematics classroom', *Journal for Research in Mathematics Education*, 51(4):399–432.

Mannion G, Sowerby M, I'Anson J (2015) *How young people's participation in school supports achievement and attainment*, Scotlands Commissioner For Children & Young People.

Marzano RJ, Marzano JS (2003) 'The key to classroom management', *Educational Leadership*, 61(1):6–13.

Merga M (2020) 'How can school libraries support student wellbeing? Evidence and implications for further research', *Journal of Library Administration*, 60(6):660–673.

Murray C, Greenberg MT (2000) 'Children's relationship with teachers and bonds with school an investigation of patterns and correlates in middle childhood', *Journal of School Psychology*, 38(5):423–445.

Nadge AJ (2005) 'Academic care: building resilience, building futures', *Pastoral Care in Education*, 23(1):28–33.

Pianta RC, Hamre BK (2009a) 'Classroom processes and positive youth development: conceptualizing, measuring, and improving the capacity of interactions between teachers and students', *New Directions for Youth Development*, 2009(121):33–46.

Pianta RC, Hamre BK (2009b) 'Conceptualization, measurement, and improvement of classroom processes: standardized observation can leverage capacity', *Educational Researcher*, 38(2):109–119.

ReachOut (2022) *Wellbeing Fives*, ReachOut website, accessed 26 January 2023. https://schools.au.reachout.com/wellbeing-5s

Reddy R, Rhodes JE, Mulhall P (2003) 'The influence of teacher support on student adjustment in the middle school years: a latent growth curve study', *Development and Psychopathology*, 15(1):119–138.

Resnick MD, Bearman PS, Blum RW, Bauman KE, Harris KM, Jones J, Tabor J, Beuhring T, Sieving RE, Shew M, Ireland M, Bearinger LH, Udry JR (1997) 'Protecting adolescents from harm: findings from the National Longitudinal Study on Adolescent Health', *JAMA*, 278(10):823–832.

Rimm-Kaufman SE, Baroody AE, Larsen RA, Curby TW, Abry T (2015) 'To what extent do teacher–student interaction quality and student gender contribute to fifth graders' engagement in mathematics learning?', *Journal of Educational Psychology*, 107(1):170.

Roorda DL, Koomen HMY, Spilt JL, Oort FJ (2011) 'The influence of affective teacher-student relationships on students' school engagement and achievement: a meta-analytic approach', *Review of Educational Research*, 81:493–529.

Skinner E, Kindermann T, Connell J, Wellborn J (2009) *Engagement and disaffection as organisational constructs in the dynamics of motivational development*, edited by Wenzel KR, and Wigfield A, Routledge, New York.

Smith C, Cahill H, Crofts J (2017) *Enhancing student wellbeing: a review of research for Catholic Education Melbourne*, Youth Research Centre, Melbourne Graduate School of Education, University of Melbourne, Melbourne.

Solomon D, Battistich V, Kim D-i, Watson M (1996) 'Teacher practices associated with students' sense of the classroom as a community', *Social Psychology of Education*, 1(3):235–267.

Swan P (2021) 'The lived experience of empathic engagement in elementary classrooms: implications for pedagogy', *Teaching and Teacher Education*, 102:103324.

Vandenbroucke L, Spilt J, Verschueren K, Piccinin C, Baeyens D (2018) 'The classroom as a developmental context for cognitive development: a meta-analysis on the importance of teacher–student interactions for children's executive functions', *Review of Educational Research*, 88(1):125–164.

Wang M-T, Brinkworth M, Eccles J (2013) 'Moderating effects of teacher–student relationship in adolescent trajectories of emotional and behavioral adjustment', *Developmental Psychology*, 49(4):690.

Wang M-T, Eccles JS (2012) 'Social support matters: longitudinal effects of social support on three dimensions of school engagement from middle to high school', *Child Development*, 83(3):877–895.

Wang M-T, Hofkens T, Ye F (2020) 'Classroom quality and adolescent student engagement and performance in mathematics: a multi-method and multi-informant approach', *Journal of Youth and Adolescence*, 49(10):1987–2002.

Wang M-T, L. Degol J, Amemiya J, Parr A, Guo J (2020) 'Classroom climate and children's academic and psychological wellbeing: a systematic review and meta-analysis', *Developmental Review*, 57:100912.

Wang M-T, Selman RL, Dishion TJ, Stormshak EA (2010) 'A Tobit Regression Analysis of the covariation between middle school students' perceived school climate and behavioral problems', *Journal of Research on Adolescence*, 20(2):274–286.

Wigelsworth M, Verity L, Mason C, Qualter P, Humphrey N (2022) 'Social and emotional learning in primary schools: a review of the current state of evidence', *British Journal of Educational Psychology*, 92(3):898–924.

CHAPTER 5

Enabling student voice and participation for wellbeing: nothing about me without me

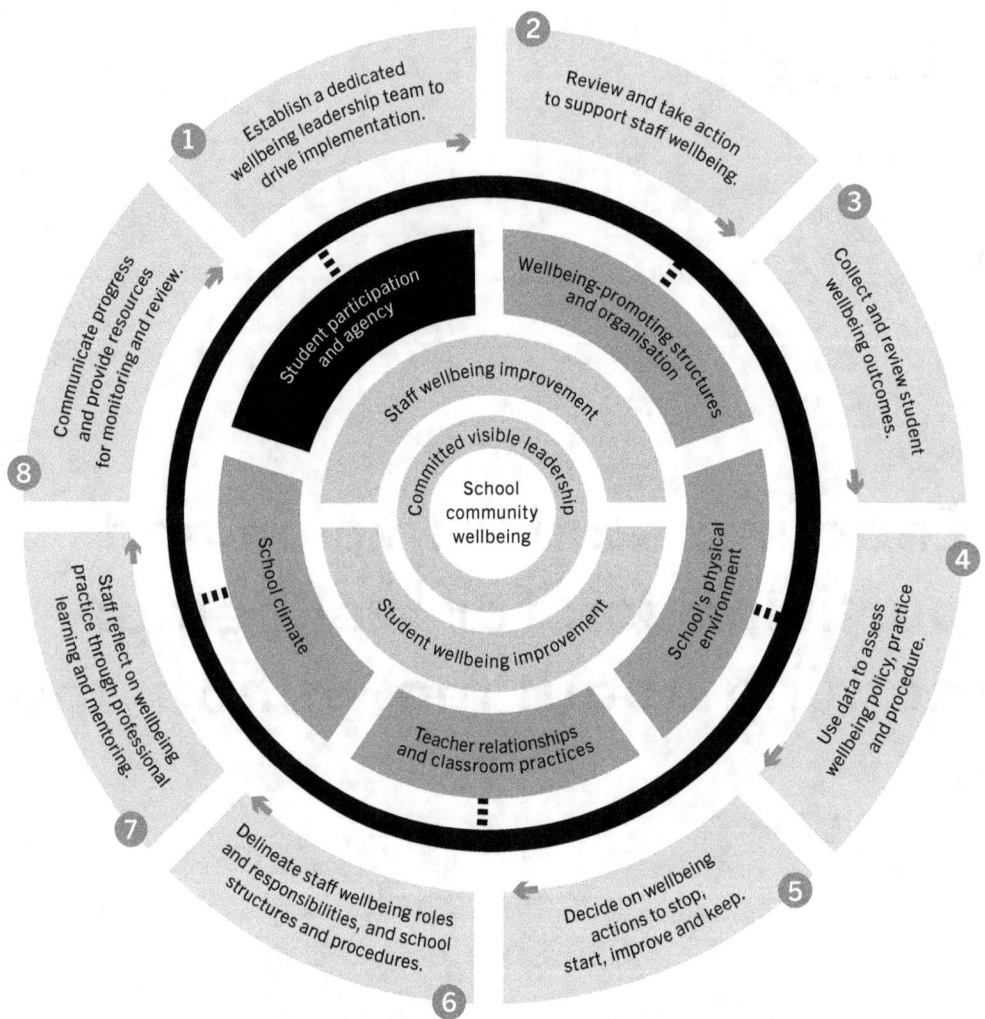

Figure 5.1. Student participation and agency

Enabling authentic student voice and participation is much more than allowing students to express their opinions and telling them that their voices matter. It's about school leadership encouraging and facilitating developmentally appropriate opportunities to genuinely engage with and listen to students and respect their contribution, to ensure they can influence decisions about matters that affect them. It requires meaningful and respectful relationships between staff and students that enable shared contributions, where students are encouraged to have choice about things that matter to them, make recommendations and have their views heard about school policies, practices and systems, work collaboratively with staff and other students, and to influence academic, wellbeing and other school-based decision-making (Cook-Sather 2006; Cook-Sather 2002; Easton 2005).

Participation needs practice

Given authentic student voice and participation is positively associated with student wellbeing (Anderson et al. 20022), school leaders need to ensure policies are in place that encourage and support all students to learn and practise with adults how to meaningfully and collaboratively contribute to projects that directly affect their lives. Proactive student participation may require a shift in staff mindset, as well as policy and practice regarding the status of students, and recognition of their capacity to be more actively involved in their education (Simmons et al. 2015). Whole-school policies that enable students, peer leaders, student action groups or students leading community service to contribute to school matters not only encourage student participation but also help students feel more ownership over their learning environment (Mitra and Gross 2009). Engaging student participation and voice also provides useful insight into what students perceive is working and not working for them at school (Osterman 2000) and improves the success of school reform efforts (Mitra 2004).

Like learning any skill, it is unrealistic to expect students to be ready for participation when they reach a certain age. They need scaffolding to learn what participation means and the rights and responsibilities involved. They need opportunities to practise and become skilled through their involvement with competent, caring adults, to ensure their contributions are appropriate, relevant, effective and sustainable.

The call for children's participation in their education is clear in Article 12 of the *Convention on the Rights of the Child*:

Parties shall assure to the child who is capable of forming his or her own views the right to express those views freely in all matters affecting the child, the views of the child being given due weight in accordance with the age and maturity of the child. (Lundy 2007: 927)

Using the Lundy (2007) model of child participation, this UN article conceptualises a child's right to participation via 4 mechanisms:

> Space (safe and inclusive opportunities to form and express views)

> Voice (being able to express ideas or opinions)

> Audience (being listened to)

> Influence (actions resulting from their participation).

Some school staff may underestimate children's ability to effectively participate via these 4 mechanisms. Just over half (55%) of the schools in a Western Australian study, for example, reported involving students in decision-making sometimes or regularly (Waters et al. 2010). In both the first and second year of secondary school, the students whose schools actively involved them in decision-making reported significantly higher feelings of school connectedness, compared to those in schools that didn't involve students in decision-making.

What does authentic student voice and participation look like?

Many school reforms in Australia recognise how authentic student voice and participation can improve the effectiveness of schools, by better meeting students' needs, improving student–staff and student–student relationships and academic achievement (De Róiste et al. 2012). A useful 'model of participation' developed by Shier (2001) provides a guide to considering the extent of student participation in schools and helps to consider the role of adults in supporting students' formal and informal participatory processes. The model comprises 5 levels of student participation that can be integrated into the culture and practices of schools. These levels help to assess if students:

> are listened to
> are supported to express their views
> have their views considered
> are involved in decision-making processes
> share the power and responsibility for decision-making.
(Shier 2001)

Shier's (2001) model also gives a temporal sequence of 15 questions (see Figure 5.2) that can be used by school staff to plan for student participation, where for each of the 5 levels, 3 stages of commitment are identified: openings (an opportunity for change might not exist yet); opportunities (where resources such as staff time, knowledge, skills and organisational capacity exist); and obligations (when policies and other commitments are made by schools to involve student participation).

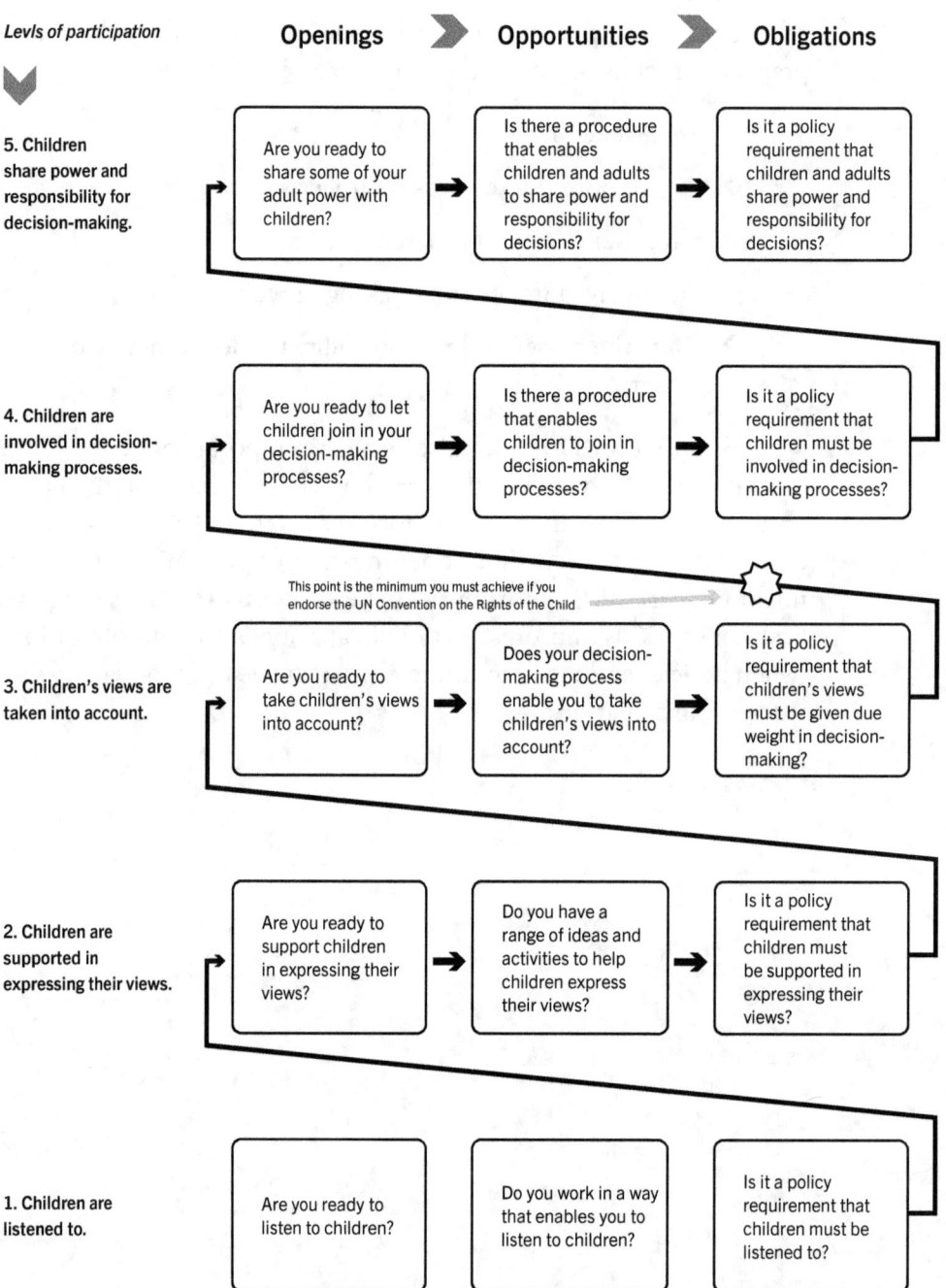

Figure 5.2. Levels of participation: 15 questions

Reproduced with permission: Shier H (2001) 'Pathways to participation: a new model for enhancing children's participation in decision making', *Children and Society*, 15(2):107–117.

Qualitative research by Anderson and Graham (2016) found that genuine student–staff communication and collaboration helps students to feel a sense of equality, safety and respect. The subsequent enhanced behavioural, cognitive and emotional engagement allows students to influence and be influenced by their school environment (Rudduck and Flutter 2000), which in turn improves their motivation, participation and feelings of self-determination (Brooks and Young 2011). Increasing student voice also helps to re-engage alienated students by providing them with a stronger sense of ownership in their schools (Oldfather 1995).

Participation, recognition and wellbeing

Empirical evidence from 3 large studies, one with over 10,000 secondary school students from Ireland (De Róiste et al. 2012), one with almost 1,500 secondary school students from Australia (Anderson et al. 2022) and one involving almost 4,000 Irish primary school students (Lloyd and Emerson 2017), found an association between high student participation at school (e.g. students are encouraged to express their views in class and participate in organising school events and making school rules) and their wellbeing (self-rated health, life satisfaction and happiness) and academic achievement – compared to students with lower level participation (e.g. those only expressing opinions about school activities). Hence, school leaders need to extend actions beyond students *only* expressing opinions, to enabling students' decision-making, influence and meaningful collaboration with peers and teachers to maximise the impact of student participation on their wellbeing and academic achievement (Mannion et al. 2015). Positive relationships between staff and students also have a critical influence on both higher levels of student participation and wellbeing (Lloyd and Emerson 2017).

Amplifying and actioning student voice and participation also enhances students' sense of recognition at school (giving and receiving care, respect and valuing others), which in turn mediates their wellbeing (Anderson et al. 2022, Graham et al. 2014). That is, increased student participation leads to increased student recognition, which in turn improves student wellbeing.

Researchers suggest that teachers can use 'recognition practices' to improve student wellbeing. Graham et al. (2014) offer the following examples:

> calling students by name and acknowledging students when seeing them

> proactively building rapport and getting to know students through attentive listening

> asking considered questions

> using pedagogical approaches that are flexible and can be adapted to the unique differences in students

> building parent–teacher relationships (working together to support students, such as including students in parent–teacher meetings)

> engaging participation and voices of the full diversity of students (elected student groups can underrepresent different cultural and marginalised students).

Bron and Veugelers (2014) suggest:

> involving students as co-designers of items such as curriculum, policy or school master plans to improve the relevance and effectiveness of these documents for the full diversity of students.

To strengthen student wellbeing, school leaders need to identify whether, how and in which contexts student voice and participation initiatives can promote their sense of recognition and consequently improve wellbeing (Anderson et al. 2022).

Autonomy, belonging and competence are critical outcomes from student participation

A learning environment that fosters and sustains students' autonomy, belonging and competence can significantly impact their motivation, engagement, achievement and wellbeing (Ryan and Deci 2017) and provide capabilities students need to succeed at school and into the future (Mitra 2004).

The 3 psychological needs, which self-determination theory (SDT) links to students' motivation and engagement, are defined as follows:

> Autonomy/agency: having influence in given situations; making decisions and choices; being able to articulate opinions to others; having a greater sense of confidence and ownership; students having an active role in their learning; and having an increased sense of responsibility to help others

> Belonging/relatedness: having meaningful relationships with other students and caring staff at school; having a strong sense of connectedness and belonging to school, home and community

> Competence: developing new capabilities and being appreciated for abilities and decision-making skills. (Deci and Ryan 2000; Deci and Ryan 2004; Ryan and Deci 2000; Van den Broeck et al. 2006; Niemiec and Ryan 2009)

In the context of schools, self-determination theory posits that students are more able to make choices and manage their life and wellbeing when they can satisfy their needs for autonomy, belonging and competence.

Autonomy

High autonomy is associated with student motivation, engagement and achievement and lower dropout rates. Conversely, students with a lower sense of autonomy are more likely to report negative psychosocial outcomes including higher levels of anxiety (Van Ryzin et al. 2009).

Students' sense of autonomy and competence is enhanced by trusted school staff who facilitate classroom practices and structures that:

> are student-centred and promote peer involvement (Watson and Benson 2008; Halliday et al. 2019)

> are shaped by student participation, ideas and initiatives (Watson and Benson 2008; Halliday et al. 2019)

> are proactive and focused on providing learning opportunities and challenges (Reeve 2016)

> develop students' intrinsic motivational skills (Reeve 2016)

> identify and nurture students' needs, interests and preferences (Jang et al. 2010)

> emphasise efforts versus ability (Jang et al. 2010)

> present interesting, relevant and enriched activities (Jang et al. 2010)

> provide flexible learning spaces to enable student-centred learning, student autonomy, self-regulation, engagement and collaboration (Kariippanon et al. 2018)

> provide clear expectations and direction towards goals to be achieved and provide help, advice and instruction to facilitate achievement of those goals (Wentzel 2016)

> are emotionally safe, supportive and nurturing, fostering expectations of high achievement (Wentzel 2016).

Other organisational and procedural actions teachers can take to support student autonomy include enabling students to provide input by choosing group members, seating, topics for units of work or types of projects. Cognitive autonomy can be enabled by students having an active role in and taking ownership of their learning and by asking them to find multiple solutions and to justify their work (Stefanou et al. 2004).

Relationships are critical to all aspects of student functioning, as they support and reinforce student autonomy and shape students' intrinsic motivation (Guay et al. 2001) and prosocial behaviour (Allen et al. 2018). As addressed in Chapter 3, enabling positive teacher–student and student–student relationships and a democratic classroom culture where students feel safe and secure expressing their thoughts and opinions (Anderson and Graham 2016) is key to student wellbeing. In Manion et al.'s (2015) study, students reported that their relationships with teachers were important for supporting their participation, influencing change in the school, and achievement. Interactions need to include informal conversations, as well as listening to students to build trust and rapport, and feelings of safety, acceptance and confidence.

Belonging

Students need to feel they belong. They need to feel safely and positively connected to school staff and peers and school experiences in general. This is especially relevant to student-teacher relationships so that students feel accepted, respected, included and supported by peers and teachers, with opportunities to learn from one another (Deci and Ryan 2004; Ryan and Deci 2000; Goodenow and Grady 1993; Baumeister and Leary 2017).

The Australian Temperament Project found that how students felt about their school was significantly related to their social competence, life satisfaction, trust of others in the community, trust in authority and to taking on civic responsibilities (O'Connor et al. 2011). Other research found students' feelings about their school also helped facilitate their transition into adulthood (Tanti et al. 2011).

Students who feel a sense of belonging and attachment to the school community are more engaged and motivated to learn (Goodenow 1993; Battistich et al. 1997), perform and achieve academically (Abdollahi et al. 2020) and have higher levels of emotional wellbeing (Arslan 2018; Arslan 2021; Arslan and Allen 2021).

Belonging and experiencing caring for others is also essential for students' psychological functioning, adjustment and wellbeing and reduces the likelihood of developing mental health difficulties, by enhancing their resilience and reducing bullying, risk-taking and disruptive behaviours (Arslan 2018; Oldfield et al. 2018; Arslan 2021).

Buhrmester (1990) argues that relatedness and belonging become especially important as children enter adolescence, where their ability to maintain positive relationships is linked to higher levels of sociability and self-esteem and increased self-efficacy, as well as reduced hostility, anxiousness and depression. In contrast, negative experiences of belonging during adolescence can have a profound effect on students' psychosocial adjustment (Allen et al. 2014). Motivational and regulatory processes can become maladaptive and harm wellbeing, which can disconnect them from school and peers (O'Brennan and Furlong 2010). This is particularly evident in middle adolescence when student disconnection from schools and peers is more prevalent (Tanti et al. 2011).

Research conducted since 2011 has found the strongest predictors of students' sense of school belonging include:

> students' connectedness to their family (St-Amand et al. 2017)
> fewer classroom and peer difficulties (St-Amand et al. 2017)
> positive transition to secondary school (St-Amand et al. 2017)
> fewer emotional problems and greater prosocial skills (St-Amand et al. 2017)
> having teachers who had positive personal characteristics and provided support (Allen et al. 2018)
> being in a school that prioritised student wellbeing and academic achievement (Cross et al. 2011).

Parent, peer and teacher support are each strongly related to school belonging, highlighting the importance of building positive school communities and engaging the positive influence of significant others. Other activities that can foster students' sense of belonging at the whole-school and classroom level include:

- encouraging student autonomy
- using cooperative learning activities to facilitate a safe, supportive and accepting environment
- providing teacher support through instructional and academic care
- using classroom pedagogy that encourages positive peer interaction and support
- facilitating multiple school friendships and the quality of those friendships
- having high expectations of each student
- using fair, non-punitive and consistent classroom and disciplinary policies and practices
- creating a safe, trusting classroom
- considering students' strengths and needs through student-centred teaching
- building well-developed social and emotional skills for successful teacher–student and peer-to-peer connections and relationships
- encouraging student participation in extracurricular activities – although more evidence is needed to understand the optimal number and type of activities.

Competence

When a student feels competent, they feel confident in their ability to do a given task that is important to them. This means they feel they have sufficient intellect, knowledge, judgment, skill and/or strength to interact effectively within their environment. The more competent a student feels, the more likely they will put in effort, persevere, challenge themselves, feel proud and approach tasks positively and with less anxiety (Bandura 1997).

Students' feelings of competence are increased when they have:

> opportunities to practise their skills, with challenges matched to their abilities.

> prompt, positive (constructive) feedback to help them feel good about their effort and what they have achieved

> opportunities to learn from and celebrate their mistakes

> tasks that help them to feel useful and competent

> opportunities to build resilience by solving problems on their own

> the ability to internalise positive self-talk

> teachers who reinforce and value student effort, not outcomes

> learning activities that are relevant to their current knowledge and interests

> learning activities that provide them with optimal challenge (not too hard or too easy).

Support to build a student's sense of competence is important from an early age, as their perceptions of competence become more stable and more resistant to change over time.

Leadership practice idea: case study

The Cyber Friendly Schools project engaged and trained Year 10 students as cyber leaders to co-design resources to support the cyber education of younger secondary school students. The 'cyber leaders' were provided with resources and support to help build and develop their leadership and planning skills to implement activities within their school that would encourage students to engage in safer, more positive and responsible cyber-related behaviour. The leaders were supported by school staff who encouraged and enabled the leaders to engage in at least one whole-school positive action per term with their younger peers (i.e. Year

7, 8 and 9 students). These actions were selected and developed by the leaders, with support, where needed, from their teachers.

The training built student capacity in 4 key areas: service leadership; using technology for good; positively influencing peers; and team building skills to promote positive action in schools. These topics are supported by an online cyber leaders' resource.

School staff were also trained and given resources to help them to assist the school leaders to lead whole-school initiatives to promote safe, positive and responsible cyber-related behaviour and strategies.

As a result of this research initiative and the impact of this positive student-led activity, a number of schools have added a senior school cyber leader to their Year 12 student leadership team alongside other school prefects/captains for sport, the arts etc.

Chapter summary

According to self-determination theory, students' need for autonomy, belonging and competence are inter-related and all 3 are required for students to experience positive wellbeing (Ryan and Deci 2000). Therefore, for students to reap benefit from their active participation in decision-making at school, they need to feel like they belong, have agency *and* a sense of competency. If the school environment meets some of these needs but not others (for example, if students don't feel like they belong) students will feel less competent and less safe in their autonomy, which will negatively impact their wellbeing.

It is critical for school leadership to create a visible commitment to a student-centred school that meaningfully encourages students to contribute as advocates, decision-makers, educators, researchers and planners. Students as active consumers in schools need to be genuinely involved in school decision-making and planning. As Cook-Sather (2002:3) stated, 'There is something fundamentally amiss about building and rebuilding an entire system without consulting at any point those it is ostensibly designed to serve'. Authentic and sustainable student participation requires collaborative relationships between teachers and students to build students' trust, confidence and capacity to engage in school decision-making. Genuine student participation ensures more democratic, participatory and inclusive decisions and actions are taken to improve the school community's wellbeing.

There are many high-impact whole-school actions that engage student participation and voice that can increase students' sense of autonomy, belonging and competence. The following indicators can be used to identify opportunities where student voice and participation can be developed and supported by the assumption that school policy and practice related to student wellbeing will be more effective if it is based on the views and ideas of students.

To improve student choice, voice, participation and decision-making we:	Not in place	Working towards	In place	Progressing well
Provide recognition to students for their ideas, opinions, feelings and actively integrate their input where possible.				
Welcome, enable and expect authentic student choice, decision-making and leadership.				
Ensure students' needs are met by engaging students as contributing stakeholders in teaching and learning, e.g. as peer educators/leaders/mentors and through community service.				
Embed strategies to ensure all students have voice safety in school decision-making, especially students from diverse backgrounds.				
Receive professional learning opportunities to enhance teacher active listening and teaching of social and emotional skills.				
Engage with each student by: • knowing their name • listening well and encouraging their choice and discussion • learning their strengths, needs, goals and connections with other students • offering help as needed.				
Provide academic and instructional support by: • providing a variety of learning activities and pedagogy aligned with student motivation and interests • encouraging students to engage and to take initiative • checking for understanding, explaining relevance and giving examples.				
Encourage positive relationships and support between peers by using interactive and cooperative learning activities, where students can develop common interests with peers.				
Establish cross-age activities, such as: • house and homeroom structures • school buddy systems or mentorships.				
Enable collaborative and inclusive communities (including engagement with parents) that encourage active student participation, focus on relationships, build connectedness and enhance cultural security.				
Engage students in extracurricular activities to provide opportunities for students to develop close relationships and common interests with peers and staff.				
Collaborate with students to co-develop strategies to enhance wellbeing, promote safety and counter antisocial behaviours in all online and physical spaces.				
Have a deep understanding of marginalised students' interests, strengths and needs.				

References

Abdollahi A, Panahipour S, Akhavan Tafti M, Allen KA (2020) 'Academic hardiness as a mediator for the relationship between school belonging and academic stress', *Psychology in the Schools*, 57(5):823–832.

Allen K, Kern ML, Vella-Brodrick D, Hattie J, Waters L (2018) 'What schools need to know about fostering school belonging: a meta-analysis', *Educational Psychology Review*, 30(1):1–34.

Allen KA, Ryan T, Gray DL, McInerney DM, Waters L (2014) 'Social media use and social connectedness in adolescents: the positives and the potential pitfalls', *The Educational and Developmental Psychologist*, 31(1):18–31.

Anderson DL, Graham AP (2016) 'Improving student wellbeing: having a say at school', *School Effectiveness and School Improvement*, 27(3):348–466.

Anderson DL, Graham AP, Simmons C, Thomas NP (2022) 'Positive links between student participation, recognition and wellbeing at school', *International Journal of Educational Research*, 111:101896.

Arslan G (2018) 'Understanding the association between school belonging and emotional health in adolescents', *International Journal of Educational Psychology*, 7(1):21–41.

Arslan G (2021) 'School belongingness, well-being, and mental health among adolescents: exploring the role of loneliness', *Australian Journal of Psychology*, 73(1):70–80.

Arslan G, Allen K-A (2021) 'School victimization, school belongingness, psychological well-being, and emotional problems in adolescents', *Child Indicators Research*, 14(4):1501–1517.

Bandura A (1997) *Self-efficacy: the exercise of control*, W.H. Freeman and Company, New York.

Battistich V, Solomon D, Watson M, Schaps E (1997) 'Caring school communities', *Educational Psychologist*, 32(3):137–151.

Baumeister RF, Leary MR (2017) 'The need to belong: desire for interpersonal attachments as a fundamental human motivation', *Interpersonal Development*, 57–89.

Bron J, Veugelers W (2014) 'Why we need to involve our students in curriculum design: five arguments for student voice', *Curriculum and Teaching Dialogue*, 16(1/2):125.

Brooks CF, Young SL (2011) 'Are choice-making opportunities needed in the classroom? Using self-determination theory to consider student motivation and learner empowerment', *International Journal of Teaching and Learning in Higher Education*, 23(1):48–59.

Buhrmester D (1990) 'Intimacy of friendship, interpersonal competence, and adjustment during preadolescence and adolescence', *Child Development*, 61(4):1101–1111.

Cook-Sather A (2002) 'Authorizing students' perspectives: toward trust, dialogue, and change in education', *Educational Researcher*, 31(4):3–14.

Cook-Sather A (2006) 'Sound, presence, and power: "student voice" in educational research and reform', *Curriculum Inquiry*, 36(4):359–390.

Cross D, Monks H, Hall M, Shaw T, Pintabona Y, Erceg E, Hamilton G, Roberts C, Waters S, Lester L (2011) 'Three-year results of the Friendly Schools whole-of-school intervention on children's bullying behaviour', *British Educational Research Journal*, 37(1):105–129.

De Róiste A, Kelly C, Molcho M, Gavin A, Gabhainn SN (2012) 'Is school participation good for children? Associations with health and wellbeing', *Health Education*, 112(2):88–104.

Deci EL, Ryan RM (2000) 'The "what" and "why" of goal pursuits: human needs and the self-determination of behavior', *Psychological Inquiry*, 11(4):227–268.

Deci EL, Ryan RM (2004) *Handbook of self-determination research*, University Rochester Press, New York.

Easton LB (2005) 'Democracy in schools: truly a matter of voice', *English Journal*, 52–56.

Goodenow C (1993) 'Classroom belonging among early adolescent students: Relationships to motivation and achievement', *The Journal of Early Adolescence*, 13(1):21–43.

Goodenow C, Grady KE (1993) 'The relationship of school belonging and friends' values to academic motivation among urban adolescent students', *The Journal of Experimental Education*, 62(1):60–71.

Graham A, Fitzgerald R, Powell MA, Thomas N, Anderson DL, White NE, Simmons CA (2014) *Improving approaches to wellbeing in schools: what role does recognition play?, Final report: volume two*, Centre for Children and Young People, Southern Cross University, Lismore.

Guay F, Boggiano AK, Vallerand RJ (2001) 'Autonomy support, intrinsic motivation, and perceived competence: conceptual and empirical linkages', *Personality and Social Psychology Bulletin*, 27(6):643–650.

Halliday AJ, Kern ML, Garrett DK, Turnbull DA (2019) 'The student voice in well-being: a case study of participatory action research in positive education', *Educational Action Research*, 27(2):173–196.

Jang H, Reeve J, Deci EL (2010) 'Engaging students in learning activities: it is not autonomy support or structure but autonomy support and structure', *Journal of Educational Psychology*, 102(3):588.

Kariippanon KE, Cliff DP, Lancaster SL, Okely AD, Parrish A-M (2018) 'Perceived interplay between flexible learning spaces and teaching, learning and student wellbeing', *Learning Environments Research*, 21(3):301–320.

Könings KD, Seidel T, van Merriënboer JJ (2014) 'Participatory design of learning environments: integrating perspectives of students, teachers, and designers', *Instructional Science*, 42(1):1–9.

Lloyd K, Emerson L (2017) '(Re) examining the relationship between children's subjective wellbeing and their perceptions of participation rights', *Child Indicators Research*, 10(3):591–608.

Lundy L (2007) '"Voice" is not enough: conceptualising Article 12 of the United Nations Convention on the Rights of the Child', *British Educational Research Journal*, 33(6):927–942.

Mannion G, Sowerby M, I'Anson J (2015) *How young people's participation in school supports achievement and attainment*, Scotlands Commissioner For Children & Young People.

Mitra DL (2004) 'The significance of students: can increasing "student voice" in schools lead to gains in youth development?', *Teachers College Record*, 106(4):651–688.

Mitra DL, Gross SJ (2009) 'Increasing student voice in high school reform: building partnerships, improving outcomes', *Educational Management Administration & Leadership*, 37(4):522–543.

Niemiec CP, Ryan RM (2009) 'Autonomy, competence, and relatedness in the classroom: applying self-determination theory to educational practice', *Theory and Research in Education*, 7(2):133–144.

O'Connor M, Sanson A, Hawkins MT, Letcher P, Toumbourou JW, Smart D, Vassallo S, Olsson CA (2011) 'Predictors of positive development in emerging adulthood', *Journal of Youth and Adolescence*, 40(7):860–874.

O'Brennan LM, Furlong MJ (2010) 'Relations between students' perceptions of school connectedness and peer victimization', *Journal of School Violence*, 9(4):375–391.

Oldfather P (1995) 'This issue: learning from student voices', *Theory Into Practice*, 34(2):86–87.

Oldfield J, Stevenson A, Ortiz E, Haley B (2018) 'Promoting or suppressing resilience to mental health outcomes in at risk young people: the role of parental and peer attachment and school connectedness', *Journal of Adolescence*, 64:13–22.

Osterman KF (2000) 'Students' need for belonging in the school community', *Review of Educational Research*, 70(3):323–367.

Reeve J (2016) 'A grand theory of motivation: why not?' *Motivation and Emotion*, 40(1):31–35.

Rudduck J, Flutter J (2000) 'Pupil participation and pupil perspective: "carving a new order of experience"', *Cambridge Journal of Education*, 30(1):75–89.

Ryan R, Deci E (2017) *Self-determination theory: autonomy and basic psychological needs in human motivation, social development, and wellness*, Gilford, New York.

Ryan RM, Deci EL (2000) 'Self-determination theory and the facilitation of intrinsic motivation, social development, and well-being', *American Psychologist*, 55(1):68.

Shier H (2001) 'Pathways to participation: a new model for enhancing children's participation in decision making', *Children and Society*, 15(2):107–117.

Simmons C, Graham A, Thomas N (2015) Imagining an ideal school for wellbeing: locating student voice, *Journal of Educational Change*, 16(2):129–144.

St-Amand J, Girard S, Smith J (2017) 'Sense of belonging at school: defining attributes, determinants, and sustaining strategies', *IAFOR Journal of Education*, 5(2):105–119.

Stefanou CR, Perencevich KC, DiCintio M, Turner JC (2004) Supporting autonomy in the classroom: ways teachers encourage student decision making and ownership', *Educational Psychologist*, 39(2):97–110.

Tanti C, Stukas AA, Halloran MJ, Foddy M (2011) 'Social identity change: shifts in social identity during adolescence', *Journal of Adolescence*, 34(3):555–567.

Van den Broeck A, Ferris DL, Chang C-H, Rosen CC (2006) 'A review of self-determination theory's basic psychological needs at work', *Journal of Management*, 42(5):1195–1229.

Van Ryzin MJ, Gravely AA, Roseth CJ (2009) 'Autonomy, belongingness, and engagement in school as contributors to adolescent psychological well-being', *Journal of Youth and Adolescence*, 38(1):1–12.

Waters S, Cross D, Shaw T (2010) 'Does the nature of schools matter? An exploration of selected school ecology factors on adolescent perceptions of school connectedness', *British Journal of Educational Psychology*, 80(3):381–402.

Watson M, Benson K (2008) 'Creating a culture for character', in Schwartz MJ (ed) *Effective character education: a guidebook for future educators*, McGraw Hill Higher Education, New York.

Wentzel KR (2016) 'Teacher–student relationships', in Wentzel KR, Miele DB (eds) *Handbook of motivation at school*, Routledge, New York.

CHAPTER 6

Organising the school for student wellbeing: roles and structures

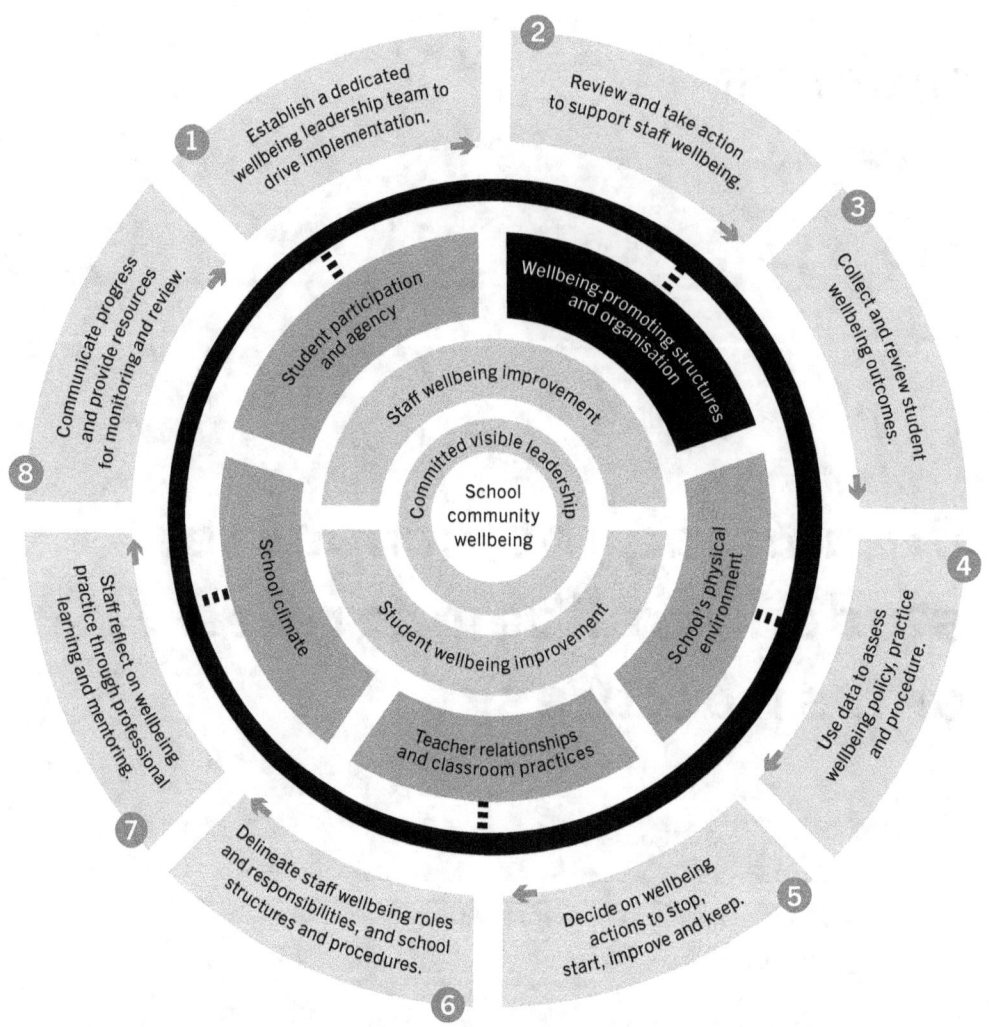

Figure 6.1. Wellbeing-promoting structures and organisation

A key priority for school leaders is building a shared vision of wellbeing and academic outcomes that avoids a structural and organisational wellbeing–academic divide, given the interdependence of these outcomes for students. An important way for school leaders to reduce this divide is to ensure their school's organisational structures support and complement wellbeing and academic care roles and responsibilities. The term 'academic care' (see Chapter 4) describes the staff actions that ensure student wellbeing and academic outcomes are deeply intwined and symbiotic.

As mentioned in other chapters, school leaders need to ensure staff clearly understand how their academic care actions, their relationships with students, and the formal and informal learning environments they create, can enhance or harm the wellbeing of students. While all staff are responsible and accountable for optimising student wellbeing, the relative intangibility of wellbeing (compared to curriculum), the lack of clarity in wellbeing roles and expectations and poorer pre-service and professional development in this area can result in staff not appreciating this is part of their role and diffusing responsibility to others.

Indeed, the sharing of responsibility for wellbeing by all staff (as well as by students, families and the broader community) is necessary to respond effectively to the increasingly complex and multifaceted nature of student wellbeing, including the growing recognition of difficulties, such as social inequalities experienced by students.

While all roles within a school need to have formalised student wellbeing responsibilities, the following positions typically have formal wellbeing or academic care roles built in to their existing position descriptions (Best 1999):

- deputy principal
- head of student wellbeing (may also be called pastoral care or student services)
- leaders of age cohorts and individual year levels
- heads of house
- head of boarding (if applicable)
- school chaplain or careers counsellor (if employed by the school)
- homeroom leaders
- behaviour support, teaching assistants and learning coordinator teachers
- psychologists and counsellors.

McLaughlin and Clarke (2010) found that to effectively promote positive student wellbeing outcomes, all school staff need to have job descriptions with KPIs that ensure staff are:

> intentional in their formal and informal interactions with all students, to build lasting, positive relationships with them

> experienced in how to promote and support student wellbeing at a group and individual level

> able to create or maximise the benefit of wellbeing learning opportunities

> purposeful in the process of ensuring support for student wellbeing difficulties.

Wellbeing and academic care champions

Schools need more than one wellbeing champion working alone. Many schools recruit an academic care or wellbeing team led by a deputy principal or equivalent level staff member to ensure wellbeing is systematically, equitably and sustainably delivered across the school. This team is best purposefully recruited to increase variability (e.g. more and less experienced staff, mixed gender and mixed learning areas) and should include interested staff and ideally, some students and parents. A committed multiskilled team, with time dedicated to this role, well informed by their own school-level data and genuinely engaged with the school community, is critical to drive wellbeing-related decision-making and action.

While historically, the deputy head/wellbeing leader role is organisationally distinct from the deputy head/curriculum leader, school leaders are recognising the value of combining this expertise or ensuring these 2 deputy roles work closely together so that students' wellbeing and academic outcomes are inextricably linked.

No matter how the leadership for wellbeing and academic care is combined, the wellbeing responsibilities must be formalised to acknowledge this complex and demanding role. The role needs to focus on driving a school culture that encourages positive relationships to optimise student learning. To successfully achieve these twin goals, school leaders need to prioritise 4 key elements:

1. Quality induction and sufficient professional learning
2. Clearly defined roles
3. Role status equivalence
4. A proactive focus on wellbeing.

1. Quality induction and sufficient professional learning

This is essential to build staff capacity (especially wellbeing leadership) and prevent burnout, as these staff respond to the increasing demands and complexities associated with student wellbeing (Ingvarson et al. 2005). Wellbeing leaders are typically appointed because they have exceptional interpersonal skills and relationships with students and other staff, with many expected to learn on the job without adequate training, time or support. While few pre-service or post-graduate education programs provide formal training in wellbeing delivery, leaders of wellbeing need specialist training to care for their own wellbeing in this role. They also need training in ways to systematically implement universal whole-school approaches to promote student wellbeing. For example, some teachers may not recognise when the appropriate time is to refer students with difficulties to others who are more qualified. Quality professional development for staff is available at the system level and also as part of programs like Be You (2023), Friendly Schools (2023) or the *Australian Student Wellbeing Framework* (ESA 2018).

2. Clearly defined roles

These will help wellbeing leaders and the school community understand what is and isn't their responsibility. The multiplicity of demands on the leaders of wellbeing means they often deal with all school matters that *aren't* curriculum related, especially if their role (unlike other roles) is poorly defined and therefore poorly understood by other staff, parents and students. Some school leaders have divided this burgeoning role into specialist areas, for example, 'head of wellbeing promotion and protection' for general wellbeing initiatives across the school and 'head of wellbeing support' for students at higher risk or students experiencing difficulties. This role separation can help, for example, to address student wellbeing confidentiality difficulties if the head of wellbeing support is also part of the school psychology or counselling team. Similarly, if all school staff have clearly defined wellbeing responsibilities, everyone has a greater appreciation for who is responsible for which actions and there is less diffusion of responsibility.

3. Role status equivalence

There exists a perception among some school staff that opportunities for further promotion are limited if they choose a wellbeing career path, compared to a career path in curriculum, and that leaders of curriculum have more positional authority than leaders of wellbeing (even when both leaders have similar experience and qualifications). The less tangible nature and impact of wellbeing leadership, compared to curriculum leadership, may be a factor related to this perception. This may mean quality staff are less likely to choose or remain on a wellbeing-related career path. School leaders need to ensure leadership roles are equitable in terms of status, resourcing, promotion and pay, to encourage quality staff to take on and remain in these important roles.

4. A proactive focus on wellbeing

The dynamic and intense nature of the wellbeing leader role means their day often involves 'putting out fires' or is derailed when new demands arise, such as a student experiencing difficulties, or behavioural concerns. They often also manage situations well outside the boundaries of their job descriptions as a key facilitator in students' multiple relationships;

for example, between the students, their teachers, their families and service providers. Wellbeing leaders are often involved in liaising with police, social workers and other family and community services when students require support or help. This work can be invisible to other staff (unless things go wrong). This intensity means leaders of wellbeing may have limited time to be proactive, relative to providing support. By ensuring the role is adequately recognised and resourced, school leaders can facilitate equitable wellbeing policies and practices to optimise every student's wellbeing, including those with high needs, and they can ensure wellbeing efforts are both proactive (wellbeing protection, promotion and prevention of problems) and reactive.

Wellbeing and academic care structures

While wellbeing roles and responsibilities in schools vary greatly, the 2 most common structures within which staff formally promote and support wellbeing are those based on the vertical streaming of students (across years), horizontal student streaming (via year levels), or a combination of both (Clark 2008; Murphy 2011). While these structures are more common in secondary than in primary school, they provide important support for both levels of schooling.

Formal wellbeing and academic care structures that might exist within a school include homeroom groups (encompassing house systems, mentor groups, houses, form room or form classes) and horizontal and vertical structures. Vertical structures can include inter-age groupings. Both horizontal and vertical structures can also involve looping, where students stay with the same peers and homeroom teachers ideally for a minimum of 3 years. Creating such structures provides interpersonal, instructional and organisational support. These structures encourage students to build more sustained and positive relationships and build student morale and subsequent school engagement. These important outcomes are best achieved by increasing the amount of time students spend with a particular teacher and group of students (same age or mixed) (Osterman 2000). All staff need to be trained in wellbeing and academic care to ensure student care is helpful, consistent and equitable across the grouping structures.

Regardless of the system used, the aim of all wellbeing and academic care structures is to foster a sense of agency, responsibility, belonging and social cohesiveness among students and to ensure every student has at least one adult in the school who is specifically responsible for building a strong relationship with, supporting and caring for them.

Homeroom groups

Wellbeing structures such as daily homeroom groups and factions/houses encourage students to build relationships and promote a sense of belonging through positive peer-to-peer student relationships (with same age as well as older and younger peers) and student-to-teacher relationships. Some school leaders avoid calling these groups 'tutor groups', as the name can suggest it has an academic support role only. Other school synonyms for 'homeroom' include mentor groups, form room and form class. Homeroom groups, as a foundation for other wellbeing and academic care structures in the school, are most effective when they are well implemented and strongly aligned with the school ethos and culture. They should be monitored and responsive to key student wellbeing outcomes (e.g. resilience and positive relationships) and evaluated regularly to ensure they are meeting students' identified strengths and needs (Robinson et al. 2009; Collins and McNiff 1999; Jamtsho 2015).

Research suggests that homeroom structures work best when the teacher-to-student ratio is low – with one homeroom teacher for groups of 15 to 20 students looped for more than one year to build more sustained relationships, especially in large schools (Day 2015). In a looping structure, students typically remain in their homeroom groups for the whole of secondary school to build stable, strong and supportive relationships between students and teachers and students and students. In Finland, for example, primary school students usually stay with the same teacher for the first 6 years of education to provide 'consistency, care and individualised attention' (Day 2015).

Vertical or horizontal?

There are advantages and disadvantages associated with homeroom groups being organised vertically or horizontally. Many schools use a horizontally structured system where students of the same year group stay together for a school year or longer, such that developmentally appropriate wellbeing and academic care strategies can target the needs of common age groups.

A horizontal 'head of year' structure is less effective compared to a cross-age 'head of house' structure in a large or growing school. Large year-level groups reduce the amount of time and equity of care heads of year can give to all students in that year group. Because of their limited time, the head of year role can become primarily reactive, focusing on student problems, rather than also being proactive and promoting wellbeing.

Further, the structure of wellbeing delivery via heads of year means these staff are not able to continue to build their relationships with students and provide continuity of care beyond one year of schooling, unless they too move with students to the next year level. Continuity of care is important to support student wellbeing, but this is less able to be provided when horizontally streamed students have a new head of year as they as they progress through school.

In contrast, a vertical homeroom system, which can be structured using ratios for both small and large schools, supports students from different year levels or clusters of year levels (e.g. Years 7-9 and 10-12, organised by house groups) and often remains intact as a group until students finish school. While house groups have traditionally enabled sporting and other co-curricular activity competitions, they also provide an important structure for continuity of care, sustained relationships and delivery of wellbeing and academic care for students if homeroom staff remain with students over time.

These mixed-age homeroom groups also enhance student safety, interpersonal skills and confidence as they enable students to form relationships with a wider variety of peers and to learn from and teach each other (Veenman 1995; Lindström and Lindahl 2011). The benefits of vertical homerooms include the opportunity for students to experience more socially relevant and natural friendships with older and younger students, cross-age role models, more peer support and stronger feelings of belonging, house identity and community. Vertical grouping has also been found to help reduce bullying and foster a greater sense of responsibility, peer mentoring, buddying and leadership skills in senior students (Murphy 2011; Thompson and Smith 2011). Given siblings are usually placed within the same houses, vertical homeroom structures also allow parents and families to have a single point of contact with their children's head of house.

A vertical homeroom structure can, however, make it more difficult to deliver developmentally based pastoral care, and older students may have a negative effect on the behaviour of younger students if the homeroom is not well led. Lastly, house structures can become so strong or unnecessarily siloed due to differential offerings or fierce competitions between houses, resulting in students identifying more closely with their 'house' than the school.

Leadership practice idea: case study

One very large inner-city secondary school's wellbeing delivery structure was organised after Year 8 with 5 houses, each with its own dean. Prior to Year 9, Year 7 and Year 8 students remained with one teacher in intact classes organised developmentally for all core learning areas and changed teachers during specialist subjects, such as PE and music. Each house had a number of vertical homerooms, each with approximately 15 students from Year 9 to 12. All staff were invited to be homeroom teachers, including the counsellors and the principal, and were looped with their vertical homeroom group of students for subsequent years until these students completed their schooling in Year 12. The heads of house met with the homeroom teachers weekly. The school staff reported the vertical organisation of students encouraged friendships across ages and built bonds between the students and the homeroom teacher.

Primary to secondary school transition

Both horizontal and vertical homeroom care structures are particularly helpful for students transitioning from primary to secondary school, as they adapt to sometimes challenging environmental, physiological, cognitive and social changes (Hirsch and Rapkin 1987). Research conducted by Waters et al (2010) suggests that effective vertical wellbeing delivery structures are more valuable early in students' transition to secondary school. Vertical structures were found in a survey completed by students to help transitioning students feel safer, experience more peer support and feel more connected to school than students who experience a horizontal structure (Waters et al. 2010). To support students through their transition to secondary school, some schools in the 3-year Supportive Schools intervention research project (Cross et al. 2018) keep students in intact (homeroom) groups for all core subjects for 1 to 3 years, giving the homeroom teacher responsibility for students' academic, social, emotional and behavioural development and learning.

Homeroom structure

Every child needs a champion or advocate for them in the school, with some needing it even more than others. Homeroom structures provide important opportunities each day to have 'eyes-on and ready support for all students', especially in secondary schools.

While daily homeroom contact with students is most important, this frequency as well as the structure, timing, duration per session and the type of activities conducted in homerooms can vary. Even the scheduling of homerooms might be adjusted to after recess or lunch, if students see it as an opportunity to arrive late to school.

Homeroom is used by some schools for administrative activities such as checking attendance, collecting and distributing information, for announcements and homework or other checks. This time is also sometimes used for house meetings or assemblies and/or to respond to negative behaviours. School leaders need to quarantine as much as possible for this valuable teacher–student and student–student interaction time to ensure it is used to care for students' wellbeing, rather than purely for administration.

Homeroom teacher responsibilities

Homeroom teachers perform multiple roles, including role model, leader, lay counsellor and, perhaps at times, surrogate parent (Liu and Barnhart 1999). Addison (2012) describes homeroom teachers as potential 'learning heroes', emphasising their important role in a student's school experience. School leaders need to ensure the homeroom role, responsibilities and expectations are part of all staff induction processes (Addison 2012). This includes accountable KPIs linked to this role (such as those listed below) and organisational strategies that provide sufficient encouragement ('the will') and professional development support ('the skill') for homeroom teachers. Their responsibilities, given their daily contact with their homeroom students, could ideally include:

> being the staff member closest to the students and the first point of contact with parents

> 'banking positive time' with students, i.e. knowing well what is happening with each student on both personal and academic levels

> recognising and celebrating each student's differences, strengths, efforts and achievements, setting high but realistic expectations and providing positive and constructive feedback on effort

> building a sense of community and encouraging students to demonstrate care and concern for each other

> welcoming, listening, valuing and providing opportunities for students to express their opinions, suggestions and perspectives

> providing opportunities for students to express their feelings and concerns, both individually and in group discussions

> demonstrating respect and concern for students and being attentive to their needs

- enabling students in the homeroom to feel safe and comforted
- using humour and engaging in activities where students have fun interacting while they learn
- monitoring students' school experiences and wellbeing and being an active advocate and mentor for students
- being available and providing support for students, especially for students experiencing learning difficulties and/or social and emotional difficulties
- acting as an intermediary between students and disciplinary staff members
- meeting and communicating with parents and visiting students' homes, if required
- being available and having individual meetings with students
- providing authentic student leadership opportunities
- teaching social and emotional skills
- enabling students to take responsibility for their behaviour and noticing and encouraging positive behaviour.

While the tasks expected of homeroom teachers need to be determined by school leadership, to continuously improve student wellbeing and school culture, the most important role of the homeroom teacher is to use at least 15 minutes each day to:

1. interact positively and get to know every homeroom student well (both personally and academically), learn their strengths and needs and know their families through regular positive contact
2. ensure their students have meaningful and relevant shared experiences and opportunities to form positive relationships with other students during homeroom

3. foster a sense of autonomy, responsibility, school connectedness and engagement in their homeroom students (Zhang 2004).

Research by Graham et al. (2014) found that students with culturally diverse backgrounds rated the relationships they had with their teachers who cared about their wellbeing as more important to them than their relationships with their classroom teachers.

Homeroom management

To maximise the benefits of homeroom time and teacher interactions with students across the school, teachers need to consistently demonstrate fairness, understanding and respect, by genuinely involving their students in the co-development of clear and specific behavioural expectations, procedures, rules and consequences. This can include helping students to resolve conflict, helping them to take responsibility for their behaviour and noticing and encouraging positive student behaviour, such as help-seeking behaviour for themselves or others.

Homeroom teachers also need to use fun and practical learning activities, including use of relevant multimedia, to encourage students to take action to show respect, concern and support for each other, especially towards peers who may be excluded or experiencing difficulties, such as being bullied. Students need homeroom time to practise social and emotional skills, while working collaboratively, ideally in cross-age groups. They also need genuine opportunities to recognise and appreciate each other's and their group's effort, strengths and achievements.

Given administrative activities can reduce the impact of the homeroom structure on student wellbeing, online student profile portals are helpful to collate and connect many descriptors of student experiences and learning at school and to confidentially report wellbeing issues and disseminate them to staff who are authorised to know. They can also track key aspects of a students' school life, such as attendance, achievements, individual learning plans, co-curricular activities, student behaviour and consequences. This information can also be linked to medical conditions and contact details for parents.

Importantly, research suggests that maximising homeroom teacher–student and student–student contact time with a combination of wellbeing and academic care strategies and structures (such as caring homeroom teachers, house systems and co-curricular activities) is the most effective mechanism to increase students' feelings of connectedness to school and is most important when students are new to the school environment (e.g. at transition) (Waters et al. 2010).

Leadership practice idea: case study

To improve student interaction in cross-age homerooms and to reduce the workload on homeroom teachers, a school required all student members of each homeroom to lead their own group in at least one homeroom activity a term. This school allocated 20 minutes to the daily homeroom time to build student connectedness and positive engagement with the school. Students were encouraged to use media they found as a basis for discussions on themes that corresponded to the school's wellbeing program, such as resilience, integrity, friendship and respect. Homeroom teachers reviewed the selected media before it was used and helped students lead the discussion. The school developed a proforma for the discussions and homeroom teachers shared between groups the best activities their students developed. Many teachers commented that student leadership in their homerooms enhanced interactions between students and ensured discussions were contemporary and relevant, while providing interesting insight into students' media-related experiences.

Allied health services: early intervention and support

Another important wellbeing and academic care structure can be found in schools' allied health teams, which encompass school counsellors, career advisors, nurses and learning and behaviour support staff. School counsellors clearly have unique skills and opportunities afforded by schools to support students' wellbeing and even increase the early intervention skills (mental health first aid) of other school staff. (The term 'school counsellor' is used here to denote all members of the allied health team within schools who are professionally trained to support students' mental and emotional wellbeing.) Allied health 'one-stop-shop' teams need to ensure they work together to encourage and normalise student help-seeking behaviours.

Targeted wellbeing activities also need to be designed to intervene early with higher risk students or to support and help connect students experiencing difficulties to treatment services outside the school. This full spectrum of care is important, given 40% of lifetime mental health problems begin before those affected are 14 years of age and 75% begin before age 25 (AIHW 10 November 2022). Mental health difficulties also peak during adolescence, with levels of depression increasing by 60% among students as they transition from primary to high school and rates of other emotional difficulties doubling from Year 7 to 9 (Lester and Cross 2015:7). The school counsellor's role is critical to support students during this challenging developmental period and may protect students against more adverse future mental health outcomes (Shaw et al. 2019).

To provide a culturally secure holistic approach to support student wellbeing, a project called 'Solid Kids, Solid Schools, Solid Families' was co-designed by Yamaji Aboriginal Elders, young people and community members, as well as local Yamaji people. This research observed that First Nations students experience interpersonal difficulties, such as bullying, in different ways to non-Aboriginal children. Hence, community members co-developed and pilot-tested specific cultural resources, including a website (Solid Kids 2023), to develop culturally safe knowledge and skills for school staff, especially allied health and Aboriginal and Islander Education Officer (AIEO) staff, to reduce social and emotional harm to First Nations young people (Coffin et al. 2010). This research demonstrated the importance of schools involving First Nations school staff, establishing strong partnerships and working closely with First Nations agencies and families to ensure culturally relevant, inclusive and culturally safe support is provided to every student. Allied health linkages with all cultural groups in school communities are critical to serve the needs of students who experience difficulties.

Some schools also use technology (such as online or telephone meetings – even before the COVID-19 pandemic) to help students build trust and rapport and to encourage and enable students, particularly boys, to engage with their school's allied health services before meeting personally. Messaging via technology (e.g. texting to student mobile phones) has also been used to help schools to coordinate, book, check in and/or follow up on appointments. Lastly, helplines and other support information for students, staff and parents can be provided through the school portal and sent to the homepage of students' devices or via apps identified and assessed by the school to be helpful.

School leaders also need to consider, as part of their improvement planning process, the location and physical environment (e.g. sound proofing of walls) around the allied services' offices to enhance student confidentiality, comfort and accessibility. Moreover, it is important for the allied health team and other key wellbeing staff to not only be located together, but also to meet as a group regularly to discuss and prepare action/support plans for students experiencing difficulties.

Given student help-seeking behaviour is quite low, especially among male secondary school students (Cardoso et al. 2012; Lawrence et al. 2015), it is important for school leaders to allocate time and create informal opportunities for the allied health team (such as the school counsellor) to get to know the students and for students to get to know members of the health team before a difficulty may arise. This can be facilitated by having members of the allied health team join student camps, visit classrooms, present at assemblies, or participate occasionally in student co-curricular activities. Friendly Schools research found only 38% of students in Years 7–9 who were targets of bullying spoke with a school staff member about it; 53% told another adult; and 48% told a friend or sibling (Shaw et al. 2019). In other Friendly Schools research, students typically reported they didn't know or understand the roles of members of the allied health team, other than the school nurse (Cardoso et al. 2012). Hence, it is important for the allied health staff to at least be known to students (including where they are located) and for students to understand what the roles of these staff entail, to increase the likelihood of students approaching them for help.

Lastly, well established connections and relationships with external allied health and wellbeing services are needed, as school counsellors may have limited time, given the recommended counsellor–student coverage ratio of 1:500 (Australian Psychological Society 2016: 31). Some schools have created 'health hubs' on their campuses in collaboration with external health services, to give families and students easier access to comprehensive allied health services.

Chapter summary

There are many organisational structures that school leaders need to consider that optimise the delivery of wellbeing promotion and protection for all students and support those at high risk or those experiencing difficulty. This chapter has described the need for role clarity among wellbeing leaders and mechanisms to engage all staff in pastoral care structures, such as houses and homerooms and allied health teams, that ensure there are 'eyes on all students'.

This table provides a checklist of high-impact actions that school leaders can take to ensure their school organisation and structure is enhancing student wellbeing and academic outcomes.

To improve our schools' wellbeing and academic care organisation and structure we:	Not in place	Working towards	In place	Progressing well
Have a common language and have formalised student wellbeing expectations and responsibilities.				
Clearly understand the school's wellbeing leadership roles and responsibilities and how to appropriately and efficiently engage with these staff to promote and protect student wellbeing.				
Have role expectations with KPIs established to ensure staff are intentional in their formal interactions with students to build lasting positive relationships with students.				
Receive professional learning to help staff promote student wellbeing at a group and individual level.				
Encourage students to contribute to homeroom activities to build peer relationships and support.				
Are purposeful in ensuring support for students experiencing wellbeing difficulties.				
Work to enhance the synergistic relationship between student academic care and outcomes and their wellbeing.				
Are proactive and positive in our actions to foster student autonomy, responsibility and school connectedness.				
Understand the wellbeing and academic care structures (including the allied health team) within the school and how to effectively use them.				
Have committed staff who actively contribute to homeroom activities (if in this role) to ensure they know about and have 'eyes on' all their homeroom students each day.				
Proactively model fairness and develop clear expectations and procedures to support the development of student relationships with and between other homeroom students (and other students in the school).				
Provide meaningful, shared experiences for students to build relationships with older and younger age groups of students.				
Maximise homeroom time to build a sense of community and for student interactions to strengthen their relationships.				
Get to know homeroom students' families and are the first point of family contact with the school.				
Monitor homeroom students' school experiences and wellbeing and provide opportunities for students to feel safe and comforted.				

References

Addison BV (2012) 'Academic care, classroom pedagogy and the house group teacher: "making hope practical" in uncertain times', *Pastoral Care in Education*, 30(4):303–315.

AIHW (Australian Institute of Health and Welfare) (10 November 2022) 'Mental health: prevalence and impact', AIHW website, accessed 31 January 2023. https://www.aihw.gov.au/reports/mental-health-services/mental-health

Australian Psychological Society (2016) *The framework for effective delivery of school psychology services: a practice guide for psychologists and school leaders*, Australian Psychological Society Limited, Melbourne, accessed 31 January 2023. https://psychology.org.au/aps/media/resource-finder/framework-delivery-school-psych-services-practice-guide.pdf

Be You (2023) *Professional Learning*, BeYou website, accessed 30 January 2023. https://beyou.edu.au/learn

Best R (1999) 'The impact of a decade of educational change on pastoral care and PSE: a survey of teacher perceptions' *Pastoral Care in Education*; 17(2):3–13.

Cardoso P, Thomas L, Johnston R, Cross D (2012) 'Encouraging student access to and use of pastoral care services in schools', *Australian Journal of Guidance and Counselling*, 22(2):227–248.

Clark K (2008) *The pastoral academic divide: impacts and implications for pastoral care* [masters by Research thesis], Murdoch University.

Coffin J, Larson A, Cross D (2010) 'Bullying in an Aboriginal context', *The Australian Journal of Indigenous Education*, 39(1):77–87.

Collins ÚM, McNiff J (1999) *Rethinking pastoral care*, Routledge, London and New York.

Cross D, Shaw T, Epstein M, Pearce N, Barnes A, Burns S, Waters S, Lester L, Runions K (2018) 'Impact of the Friendly Schools whole-school intervention on transition to secondary school and adolescent bullying behaviour', *European Journal of Education*, 53(4):495–513.

Cross D, Runions KC, Pearce N (2021) Friendly Schools' bullying prevention research: implications for school counsellors, *Journal of Psychologists and Counsellors in Schools*, 31(2):146–158.

Day K (2015) 'In Finland, less = more', *AEU (SA Branch) Journal*, 47(3):14–16.

ESA (Education Services Australia) (2018) *Australian Student Wellbeing Framework*, Education Council, Carlton South, VIC, accessed 17 January 2023. https://studentwellbeinghub.edu.au/educators/framework

Friendly Schools (2023) *Friendly Schools* [website], accessed 26 January. https://friendlyschools.com.au/

Graham A, Fitzgerald R, Powell MA, Thomas N, Anderson DL, White NE, Simmons CA (2014) *Improving approaches to wellbeing in schools: what role does recognition play?, Final report: volume two*, Centre for Children and Young People, Southern Cross University, Lismore.

Hirsch BJ, Rapkin BD (1987) 'The transition to junior high school: a longitudinal study of self-esteem, psychological symptomatology, school life, and social support', *Child Development*, 1235–1243.

Hoy WK, Hannum JW (1997) 'Middle school climate: an empirical assessment of organizational health and student achievement', *Educational Administration Quarterly*, 33(3):290–311.

Ingvarson L, Meiers M, Beavis A (2005) 'Factors affecting the impact of professional development programs on teachers' knowledge, practice, student outcomes & efficacy', *Education Policy Analysis Archives*, 13(10).

Jamtsho S (2015) *Implementing a whole-school approach to student wellbeing: a study examining the implementation experiences of Bhutanese and Australian teachers in wellbeing leadership roles*, Melbourne Graduate School of Education, University of Melbourne.

Lawrence D, Johnson S, Hafekost J, Boterhoven de Haan K, Sawyer M, Ainley J, Zubrick SR (2015) *The mental health of children and adolescents: report on the second Australian child and adolescent survey of mental health and wellbeing*, Commonwealth of Australia, Canberra.

Lester L, Cross D (2015) 'The relationship between school climate and mental and emotional wellbeing over the transition from primary to secondary school', *Psychology of Wellbeing: Theory, Research and Practice*, 5(9):1–15.

Lindström EA, Lindahl E (2011) 'The effect of mixed-age classes in Sweden', *Scandinavian Journal of Educational Research*, 55(2):121–144.

Liu J-q, Barnhart R (1999) 'Homeroom teacher and homeroom class: the key to classroom management in China's schools', *The Educational Forum*, 63:380–384.

McLaughlin C, Clarke B (2010) 'Relational matters: a review of the impact of school experience on mental health in early adolescence', *Educational and Child Psychology*, 27(1):91.

Murphy K (2011) *The complexity of pastoral care middle leadership in New Zealand secondary schools*, [unpublished document submitted in partial fulfilment of the requirements for the degree of Master of Educational Leadership and Management], Unitec Institute of Technology, Auckland, New Zealand.

Osterman KF (2000) 'Students' need for belonging in the school community', *Review of Educational Research*, 70(3):323–367.

Robinson V, Hohepa M, Lloyd C (2009) *Best evidence synthesis. School leadership and student outcomes: identifying what works and why*, Ministry of Education, Wellington.

Shaw T, Campbell MA, Eastham J, Runions KC, Salmivalli C, Cross D (2019) 'Telling an adult at school about bullying: subsequent victimization and internalizing problems', *Journal of Child and Family Studies*, 28(9):2594–2605.

Solid Kids (2023) *Solid Kids, Solid Schools, Solid Families, Solid Kids* [website], accessed 31 January 2023. https://www.solidkids.net.au

Thompson F, Smith PK (2011) *The use and effectiveness of anti-bullying strategies in schools*, Research Report DFE-RR098, Goldsmiths, University of London, London.

Veenman S (1995) 'Cognitive and noncognitive effects of multigrade and multi-age classes: a best-evidence synthesis', *Review of Educational Research*, 65(4):319–381.

Waters S, Cross D, Shaw T (2010) 'Does the nature of schools matter? An exploration of selected school ecology factors on adolescent perceptions of school connectedness', *British Journal of Educational Psychology*, 80(3):381–402.

Zhang A (2004) 'A cross-national examination of Chinese and US classroom culture', *National Communication Association's 90th annual conference in Chicago*, accessed 30 January 2023. http://www.iiqi.org/C4QI/httpdocs/qi2005/papers/zhang.pdf

CHAPTER 7

The third teacher: the school physical environment and wellbeing

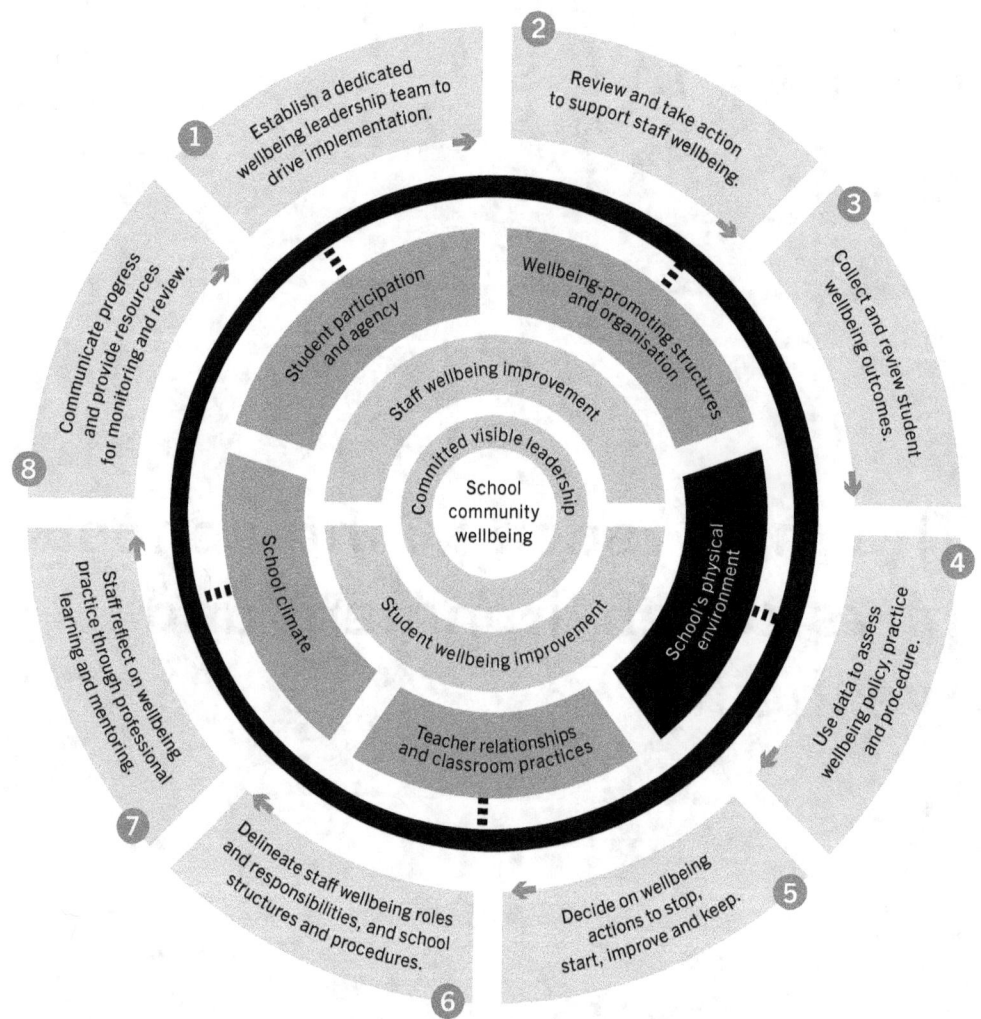

Figure 7.1. School's physical environment

Loris Maguzzi, founder of the Reggio Emilia approach, is widely attributed as saying, 'There are three teachers of children: adults, other children and their physical environment'. The physical or built environment is a powerful influence on the school community's wellbeing and is often overlooked when school leaders consider policies and practices to improve wellbeing outcomes for students, staff and families. There is growing evidence, however, that a school's physical environment can influence the school community's behaviour, sense of school connectedness and belonging, social interaction, safety and mental health, and can promote students' cognitive and non-cognitive learning (Renalds et al. 2010).

A well-structured, well-maintained, safe and healthy built environment (i.e. its physical attributes) is recognised by the World Health Organization (WHO 2004) as an essential component of a health-promoting school. The WHO (2004:1) suggests a school's physical environment comprises 'the school building and all its contents including physical structures, infrastructure, furniture, and the use and presence of chemicals and biological agents; the site on which a school is located; and the surrounding environment including the air, water, and materials with which children may come into contact, as well as nearby land uses, roadways and other hazards'.

Research shows that a poorly maintained school physical environment can reveal how much the school cares about the school community, and can impede student learning (Hoyle 1977). Hence, transdisciplinary teams of architects, health promotion practitioners, sociologists and educational researchers are collaboratively using evidence to design schools that can enhance the social and psychological safety (actual and perceived) of the school community before a school is built (Fram and Dickmann 2012). Most existing schools also have a built environment master plan, ideally developed with input from the school community, to guide the expansion, as well as the maintenance and positive use of, facilities, space, equipment and activities. Transdisciplinary evidence can provide an additional source of information to support decision-making by school leaders and their governance bodies during these master plan processes.

A built environment master plan needs to not only address ways to prevent harm and protect the safety and wellbeing of all members of the school community but should also consider how the environment itself can promote wellbeing.

In this chapter, a school's physical environment is defined as the structural, functional and built environment. Structural features include a school's sector, primary and/or secondary focus, socioeconomic status, the number of students and its size in area. Functional features include the organisation of wellbeing initiatives and strategies, such as horizontal or vertically organised house and homeroom structures (as discussed in Chapter 4), as well as how the school enables student agency, and physical features, such as artwork, the condition of equipment and outdoor areas and the presence of litter and graffiti. Students' sense of belonging can be impacted, for example, by the amount of student and other artwork featured in the school (Killeen et al. 2003).

This broad description of the school's physical environment encompasses more than what has been traditionally conceptualised as the built environment (i.e. playgrounds, buildings and gardens) and encourages school leaders to consider how the school's environment can be even more welcoming, inclusive, enriching, responsive to students' interests, strengths and needs, and can enhance their cognitive and non-cognitive (social and emotional) learning. Lackney (1999) for example, identified 9 built environment factors that can have a positive impact on student achievement:

1. crowding and spacing
2. places for social interaction
3. building functionality
4. sensory stimulation
5. personalisation and ownership
6. classroom adaptability
7. privacy
8. aesthetics and appearance (e.g. student artwork, plants)
9. physical comfort and health (e.g. fresh air, shade).

This chapter will describe key actions school leaders can take to review and renew their school's physical environment to help protect and promote the wellbeing of the school community, especially students.

What school community wellbeing outcomes are influenced by the physical environment?

The Reggio Emilia approach (Gandini 1993) shows that a school's physical environment, if functioning well, can contribute much to student learning, achievement and wellbeing, especially students' prosocial behaviour and friendships, autonomy, identity, sense of belonging and connectedness to the school (Ellis 2002; Ellis 2004; Langhout 2003; White 2004). Berner (1993) for example, found a positive relationship between the quality of the built environment and student test scores, where average achievement scores were found to increase as the school conditions improved.

Western Australian research conducted in secondary schools found an association between the following school features and higher student connectedness and mental health outcomes (compared to students whose schools didn't have these features):

> policies and practices that prioritised student wellbeing or pastoral care

> well-established house systems and vertical homeroom structures

> graffiti removed as quickly as possible (especially among students in their first year of secondary school). (Waters et al. 2010)

The school community's mental health also appears to be indirectly influenced by a physical environment that enables psychosocial processes and helps to increase a sense of autonomy or personal control, socially supportive relationships and relief from stress and fatigue (Evans 2003).

Research has identified the impact the physical environment also has on the social (and antisocial) behaviour of students. Numerous studies, including one involving 351 schools (Learning Through Landscapes 2003), reported a significant reduction in student bullying behaviour because of improvements to the school physical environment, such as identifying 'bullying hotspots' and designing more interesting and stimulating school grounds (Fite et al. 2003; Vaillancourt et al. 2010). Malone and Tranter (2003) suggest there is less conflict between students in school grounds with sufficient play equipment and enough variety in facilities to engage all students. Co-designing outdoor (and indoor) spaces with the school community is therefore critical to ensure they are relevant, well planned and well constructed. When co-designed by the users, these facilities will more likely enable and encourage students to enjoy more positive peer relationships and feel safer and more connected to their school and staff and, in turn, improve student (and staff) attendance and engagement.

Actions to improve a school's physical environment

Environmental scans and reviews

There are many actions school leaders and the school wellbeing team can take as part of reviewing and renewing their school's structural, functional and built environment to further enhance students' safety, learning outcomes and wellbeing (and possibly staff and families' wellbeing). The first and most important step is conducting ongoing and regular (annual) physical environment scans involving the school community. These environmental scans or assessments can include:

> ❯ the current use of structures, space, facilities and equipment
> ❯ staff supervision and capacity
> ❯ how students and staff feel about these features
> ❯ recommendations for improvement.

This section describes some ways to involve the school community in this physical environment scan and review, which is invaluable for leaders to ensure school policies and practices related to the school's physical environment are addressing the issues, interests and areas of greatest concern to students.

Firstly, wellbeing teams can use records of incidents or behaviours collected by their school to provide an inventory and ideas for their physical environment improvement cycle, especially if type of incident, location, time and frequency is recorded. Environmental scans could also be regularly conducted by staff in the areas they supervise during breaktimes, assessing the nature of student use, safety and interest or enjoyment. Alternatively, students can formally or informally provide feedback on the areas they use during break times that they find safe and not-so-safe or enjoyable and not-so-enjoyable. Students in each year group can use a map of the school or allocated sections of the map, as a homeroom project for example, to take photographs, and highlight or describe the areas, structures and equipment where they like spending time, those where they don't and those areas they neither like nor dislike. In a study conducted by Astor et al. (2004), school staff and students agreed after collecting and analysing these data that they needed to increase staff supervision, implement some school beautification projects and adjust student movement times to address student crowding by reducing the number of students moving around the school. All these actions helped to reduce incidents of bullying.

Leadership practice idea: case study

In one primary school, younger students were asked to colour areas on their school map in green, yellow and red, to show where they enjoy spending time (green), the areas they avoid (red) and those areas that they felt were neutral (i.e. neither enjoy nor deliberately avoid) as yellow. This school also involved staff and parents in the mapping activity, asking how they felt about the levels of safety and how much they liked or disliked areas in the school. A sub-sample of students, staff and parents who provided mapping feedback or photographs depicting these areas were then asked to describe (in small affinity groups or anonymously via a suggestion box) what about the areas made them feel the way they indicated and how these areas, structures or equipment could be improved.

School leaders also need to consider the ways the school environment enables cultural safety, opportunities for social interactions and inclusivity. For example, what elements in the school grounds are welcoming to, improve the whole school community's cultural understandings of and are supportive of First Nations and other culturally diverse families and students?

Some fundamental questions school leaders could consider as part of the school's environmental scans and response include:

> Is there enough space and equipment for students to play together positively?

> Is there equitable allocation of equipment and space that's enjoyable for all year groups and sub-groups in the school?

> Is there adequate monitoring, supervision and direction to keep students safe and to stop them from accessing out-of-bounds areas?

> Are the break-time activity options and areas sufficiently diverse to meet students' interests, strengths and needs?

> Does the school built environment display, privilege and honour students' voices and effort?

> What elements of the physical environment are welcoming, inclusive and positive to the school community and how can these be expanded?

These insights can be helpful for risk mitigation or to generate ideas to improve the structural aesthetics and safety of those environments through making difficult-to-manage areas off-limits for students or providing more comprehensive supervision. It will be important to also consider off-site physical environments, such as recreation centres, school campsites and other places where students engage in excursions. Similarly, environment master planning and physical environment assessments need to be mindful of staff facilities and their use and related wellbeing. Considerations may include areas for preparation, respite, collaboration, meetings with other staff and meetings with students, training and areas to be social with other staff.

'Hotspots'

Areas often identified by students as problematic 'hotspots' are typically isolated or less visible or poorly supervised and can include toilets, canteen areas, transition spaces (i.e. staircases, corridors, queues), outdoor play spaces (including playgrounds and courts), changerooms, classrooms and school buses (Francis et al. 2022), as well as locker areas and car parks. Research conducted by Astor et al. (2001) suggests that 'hotspots' tend to be 'unowned' by either students or school staff. This is especially the case in secondary schools, which seem to have more unowned areas because they are larger and possibly because secondary school teachers tend to be more territorially linked to their specific classrooms or learning areas.

Nevertheless, areas in schools that are less well monitored or supervised or are poorly maintained may increase the presence of physical reminders of delinquency (e.g. litter, vandalism, graffiti), which in the vein of the 'broken windows theory' (Psychology Today 2022), can make students feel unsafe and negative about the school and increase the likelihood of antisocial behaviours such as bullying (Design Council 2022). The rationale for this theory that has been shown to be true in schools is that when physical disorder is perceived to be accepted, 'informal social controls diminish' and potential offenders feel less threat of punishment. As a result, they may have an increased propensity to offend (Egli et al. 2010).

Locker areas are often identified as hotspots in school assessments, typically due to their design, which causes crowding and containment and poor staff visibility of student behaviour, plus the added constraint of time pressure on students to quickly secure what they need between classes. Most commonly, the structure of the locker rooms and the requirement for students to access these (often with lockers above and below other students) in a very limited space and time, requires considerable cooperation and goodwill on the part of students. Hence, sometimes the school's built environment alone can contribute to poor behavioural outcomes, making it an important factor for consideration by school leaders and their wellbeing committee. Modifying the built environment to be more amenable to positive student behaviour in places like locker areas and further afield in other potentially troublesome places, like the canteen line and at the bike racks, can be universal, easy to implement, 'low hanging fruit' strategies that can positively affect the lives of the whole school community and their interactions.

Wilcox et al. (2006) strongly recommend that, where possible, school leaders reduce physical disorder in school buildings and school grounds and increase school pride through actions such as hanging artwork or school banners. This research also encouraged leaders to work towards increasing supervision and surveillance in outside areas by reducing visual obstructions where possible and to enable staff supervision to enhance informal and positive social control and reduce poor behaviour.

Supervision and visibility

Given the cost of capital improvements in schools, many physical environment issues identified may need to be addressed via functional changes, such as staff supervision and boundaries and proactive or preventative actions, rather than only through modifications to a school's built environment. Bullying, for example, is more likely to occur in large spaces with few rules, where there is a high student-to-teacher ratio and limited capacity for or poor adult supervision (Fite et al. 2013).

To ensure teacher break-time supervision is fair and consistent with school policy (and therefore consistent with other staff actions), supervision induction for all new staff and annual staff training boosters are critical to ensure all staff (including relief staff) have common understandings about what is acceptable and unacceptable behaviour and what actions they are required to take in accordance with the school's policies. The consistency and fairness of responses to students between staff and by the same staff member is essential, as evidence shows student aggression and other poor behaviour will likely continue to escalate until a peer/adult/staff member intervenes (Mulryan-Kyne 2014; Cross et al. 2009). If no action is taken when students behave badly, they can assume that level of aggression or poor behaviour is condoned. Competitive activities in particular need to be well supervised, with sufficient equipment and space to encourage positive behaviour.

Reviewing staff expectations and ensuring their KPIs provide clarity about their supervision role during break times is critical. As discussed in Chapter 4, building relationships with students, especially with those less known to teachers, is an important KPI during supervision, as opposed to the role being only about keeping students safe and discouraging poor behaviour. Student supervision is an important time for school staff to build 'relationship credit' by intentionally learning more about as many students as possible, while also ensuring students are playing or spending time safely, ideally actively and interacting with others in positive ways.

Not surprisingly, places where the student-to-teacher ratio is higher during break times, such as in the library or places where more empathetic teachers are on duty, are often described as safer by students. When staff are not able to provide adequate supervision, some schools have also installed observation aids, such as CCTV and improved lighting or have cleared areas to increase student visibility.

Leadership practice idea: case study

The Friendly Schools social and emotional program research conducted in 2004 investigated the impact of increasing duty teachers' visibility by encouraging staff to wear brightly coloured vests (Cross et al. 2012). While the researchers were working in one school, they heard claims from students and parents that there were no teachers on duty during break times. In response to this claim, the researchers noticed that while there were plenty of teachers on duty, they were a similar height to students and not easily visible. The school agreed to trial the use of bright coloured vests if they were not made with Velcro that could catch on teachers' clothes. They had 'duty teacher' written on the back (so teachers weren't confused with other workers in the school) and they included a pocket for first aid items and a phone. After teachers commenced wearing these coloured vests, students reported they felt safer because they could more easily see where teachers were located. These vests are now commonly used in schools to improve student perception of safety.

The allied health team, including the school psychologist, counsellor or school nurse also plays an important functional role to support students seeking help during break times. Their office location and visibility relative to other student facilities in the school is important to ensure it is not stigmatising for students to wait near or enter the area, which may act as a barrier to student patronage (Cardoso et al. 2012). These help-seeking facilities also need to be designed to feel welcoming, positive and comfortable and should be soundproof. Further, Eliot et al. (2010) found that 44% of the student help-seeking behaviour variation among schools was accounted for by a supportive school climate, such that far more students would seek help if they perceived school staff to be caring, respectful and interested in them.

Leadership practice idea: case study

One school with an effective approach to wellbeing has a 'one-stop shop' where all allied health staff are located. To increase the use of this facility, the school promotes the normalisation of help-seeking, and encouraging students to help each other, where needed, to book appointments.

Online spaces in schools also continue to provide a unique challenge for staff, given the need for students to use the digital environment to learn and play. Like the school's physical environment, school leaders need to ensure school staff are monitoring student behaviour in online environments using co-developed school policy agreements and rules, with consequences for breaches. Structural changes, such as filtering software on school-based devices and adjusting classroom teaching and learning with support from the eSafety Commissioner website (eSafety Commissioner n.d.) can help school staff manage student behaviour in online environments, as well as help students to help themselves and others. Some school staff are also vulnerable online and will require training to reduce their risk of loss of privacy, responding to phishing, malware attacks, trolling and other cyber security risks.

Supportive school facilities and activities

School leaders need to ensure that school facilities and equipment (with good student supervision) provide positive learning experiences and that when students are using these they do not feel alienated or marginalised. A review of facilities and equipment also needs to consider the time of the year, including the quality of shade provision, access to drinking water, sunscreen and hot and wet weather alternative spaces, equipment and activities.

The most likely first contact with a school – the 'front office' – can contribute to a school community's wellbeing. It provides a memorable impression of how the school treats its community. These snap judgements may not be accurate, but they endure. The office needs to be easy to locate, warm and welcoming to all those arriving at and leaving the school. The space should be intentionally proud, showcasing the whole school community, especially cultural groups in the school, and celebrating student and staff achievements and student belonging and voice in the school.

School leaders need to be mindful of how the school environment and access to equipment and space can exacerbate or mitigate safety issues like bullying, conflict and harassment. Finding ways to encourage greater and more equitable use, distribution and return of developmentally appropriate non-fixed play equipment and facilities (e.g. balls and basketball rings) and space may require formal scheduling to reduce potential conflict, given the 'power' or dominance that can be associated with use of this equipment. In some instances, poor student behaviour was found to be caused by competition over limited resources (Horton et al. 2020). If the physical environment scan identifies small numbers of equipment or limited access to popular spaces, students' access to these areas or possession of equipment may facilitate power differences.

The availability of balls for example, has been associated with bullying behaviour. The allocation and rotation of defined spaces and shared equipment to sub-groups of students can help to limit the power that may be associated with occupying popular locations or using equipment to the exclusion of others (Francis et al. 2021). Some schools have also found that limiting equipment brought from home (which can get lost, broken or taken by others) can also reduce angst among students (Lake 2014).

Like other school equipment, outdoor seating can be powerful if limited in number and in fixed positions. Students with the most 'power' typically occupy the seats, causing other students to stand near or behind them. Non-fixed seating in sufficient numbers for demand can enable students to arrange chairs to suit the groups they are forming and can encourage conversation and facilitate more inclusive and positive interactions.

Leadership practice idea: case study

One school decided to remodel an area of bush within the school grounds that had become a rubbish trap and a place where students engaged in some antisocial behaviours. After clearing the area, the principal invited the school community to co-design the landscape and name the new area such that it encouraged positive student interaction. While the area was built with trees, fixed shade and curved walls that could be used for seating, the wellbeing team decided there would be no fixed chairs. Instead, free standing, single outdoor chairs were purchased, which students could use to form seated groups of any size that suited them. These chairs were purchased in plentiful supply to meet demand and students in the secondary school were rotated through this area to ensure all year groups would have the chance to benefit from this inviting and interesting outdoor environment that was named 'the common'.

Student break-time places, like eating areas, libraries, clubrooms and undercover areas, need to be diverse and structured (with sufficient equipment, if required) to encourage students to interact positively with other students, regulate their emotions and learn and practise their social skills. For example, some schools have 'no technology use' policies during break times to encourage face-to-face interactions, or no technology in key places where lonely children may congregate, such as libraries. Offering board games, for example, or in-school clubs, such as a chess club, are options that are often more inclusive and supportive of different student needs and that help to build positive social skills and facilitate cross-age integration. Supervised indoor activities enable vulnerable, shy and lonely students in particular, to feel safer and provide opportunities to meet other (potentially lonely) students. Ideally these activities are collaborative, with a focus on practising social skills and building reciprocated friendships, while interacting with other students (Horton et al. 2020).

Leadership practice idea: case study

Mindful of the weather, a primary school principal in Western Australia would seemingly spontaneously provide students with buckets of coloured chalk to use to draw on the asphalt in specified areas. This principal recognised this non-competitive activity, which always generated much excitement, was inclusive of all students, and he cleverly offered this activity once he had determined rain was due later in the week (to clean the area for other activities).

Schools involved in Friendly Schools research (in which the authors of this book have participated) have also identified the length of recess and lunchbreaks as a factor affecting student wellbeing. School-level behaviour data in these schools (which mostly had one-hour lunchbreaks) showed that most of the student behaviour problems were occurring towards the last 5–10 minutes of the lunchbreak. This increase in poor behaviour could have been due to student boredom from not being sufficiently engaged in activities throughout the lunchbreak. Several wellbeing teams from these schools decided to shorten the lunchbreak slightly and lengthen the morning recess break instead. These schools anecdotally reported they saw a noticeable decrease in lunchbreak behavioural problems and no change at recess.

Some schools also provide positive, comfortable and supervised areas, such as a 'breathe easy' room (e.g. with bean bags and music) open during break times for students who may be feeling uncomfortable, need somewhere to 'cool down' their emotions or who are just in need of a quiet space. Some specialist training is often required for staff working alongside students experiencing difficulties and to monitor and support students who are identified as potentially at risk.

Reducing bullying and aggression

As mentioned previously, an important consideration when reviewing the school's structural, organisational and built environment is the extent to which it is influencing student behaviour. Research by Migliaccio et al. (2017) found the features of the school built environment more likely to exacerbate bullying behaviour included architectural design and layout (e.g. isolated buildings out of teachers' sight, large distances between buildings and playgrounds), poor aesthetics (e.g. no garden beds), limited seating, absence of security cameras and vandalism.

Francis et al.'s (2022) comprehensive review of 43 studies of school bullying locations, found that the most frequently identified school bullying locations, in addition to the classroom, were the schoolyard/playground, hallways, toilets, canteen, gymnasium or changeroom and locker areas. The authors also found that more primary than secondary school students were bullied in the playground and in toilets.

School toilets and locker rooms were also identified by LGBTIQ+ students as the least safe spaces within schools, with toilets linked to the verbal, physical and sexual assault of LGBTIQ+ students (James et al. 2015; Murchison et al. 2019). Policies and practices such as the use of gender-neutral bathrooms can help prevent the bullying and other aggression directed at LGBTIQ+ students and help prevent subsequent physical and mental health problems (Francis et al. 2022). A US–Canadian study found, however, that while LGBTIQ+ students reported positive experiences using gender-neutral toilets in schools, if these toilets were located in more isolated areas of the school, they were more likely to feel stigmatised and concerned about their safety (Porta et al. 2017).

Francis et al. (2022) suggest the use of the following built environment features may help prevent bullying behaviour:

> non-fixed play equipment

> permanent student artwork in interior spaces

> anti-bullying posters

> security cameras

> replacing concrete in the schoolyard with grass or soft-fall rubber
> providing quality sports areas (e.g. basketball courts and pathways).

Similar to recommendations in Chapter 4 addressing the impact of quality student–teacher relationships on student behaviour, research (Johnson 2009) shows that schools with less student aggression and violence also tend to have students who feel that:

> they have ownership of the school environment
> the school environment is orderly
> the school rules are fair and fairly enforced
> they are in a school environment that is positive and focused on learning.

Chapter summary

This chapter describes the ways a school's physical environment (structural, functional and built) can influence students' cognitive and non-cognitive learning, sense of safety, social development, behaviour and wellbeing, and what high-impact actions related to the school's physical environment can form part of the school improvement process. School leaders are provided with examples of processes they can use to determine what high-impact practices they need to embed in the school master planning process, particularly to address school 'hotspots'. These practices, including environment reviews, staff supervision and providing supportive facilities and activities, can systematically and strategically optimise the school physical environment to ensure it is safe, highly accessible and responsive to students' developmental and cultural strengths and needs; provides fun, risk and challenge; encourages positive interactions and socialisation between students; enables physical activity and allows the school community to have a sense of ownership and belonging.

The table below provides a checklist of high-impact practices school leaders can take to ensure their school's physical environment is contributing positively to student wellbeing.

To improve our schools' structural, functional and built environment we:	Not in place	Working towards	In place	Progressing well
Engage the school community annually to identify and understand safety 'hot spots' in the school and put in place strategies to improve these.				
Understand and map how space, facilities and equipment are being used in the school environment, by whom and how students and staff feel about these features, and modify those that are poorly used or causing concern.				
Monitor to ensure equitable use and rotation of space, facilities and equipment for all student year groups.				
Identify ways the school's physical environment may evoke a sense of power in some students (e.g. access to equipment or key spaces in the school) and implement actions to minimise this risk.				
Examine the variety of competitive and non-competitive activities offered during break times to ensure they meet students' interests, needs and strengths.				
Review teacher supervision during break times to ensure adequate coverage of areas where students are located.				
Identify areas in the school that are out-of-bounds for students, i.e. where no teacher supervision can be provided or where teacher visibility of students is limited.				
Allocate specific locations and staff who can provide additional support to students who may be experiencing difficulties during break times.				
Ensure built environment features are non-stigmatising, such as the location of the allied health team or gender-neutral toilets.				
Review the school's maintenance schedule in consultation with the school's governing body to ensure an adequate budget to address needs.				

Co-design with the school community, including with a cross-section of students (i.e. not just student leaders), the school physical environment master plan to improve the structural, built and functional features of the school.				
Consider offsite and shared physical environments, such as school campsites and other places the school uses for excursions, as well as online spaces where students spend time.				
Ensure graffiti and other vandalism damage to the school is removed or repaired as soon as possible.				
Make sure the front office space, function and staffing is warm and welcoming, and is a culturally inclusive environment.				
Display student artwork and other achievements throughout the school, especially in the school leaders' offices.				
Reduce student crowding and potential for conflict in areas around the school.				
Provide sufficient quality shade and wet-weather alternative spaces during break times for student use as required.				
Provide supervision, facilities, space and equipment that encourages positive student interaction.				
Systematically record and monitor student and staff incidents involving the built environment and use these data to improve the built environment.				
Train staff as part of their induction and via regular training boosters to ensure appropriate and consistent student supervision (aligned with school duty of care policies).				
Co-design staff facilities with staff to ensure they meet their professional and wellbeing needs.				

References

Astor RA, Benbenishty R, Marachi R (2004) 'Violence in schools', in Meares PA (ed) *Social work services schools* (4th edn), Allyn & Bacon, Boston, MA.

Astor RA, Meyer HA, Pitner RO (2001) 'Elementary and middle school students' perceptions of violence-prone school subcontexts', *The Elementary School Journal*, 101(5):511–528.

Berner MM (1993) 'Building conditions, parental involvement, and student achievement in the District of Columbia public school system', *Urban Education*, 28(1):6–29.

Cardoso P, Thomas L, Johnston R, Cross D (2012) 'Encouraging student access to and use of pastoral care services in schools', *Australian Journal of Guidance and Counselling*, 22(2):227–248.

Cross D, Shaw T, Hearn L, Epstein M, Monks H, Lester L, Thomas L (2009) *Australian covert bullying prevalence study*, Child Health Promotion Research Centre, Edith Cowan University, Perth, Australia.

Cross D, Waters S, Pearce N, Shaw T, Hall M, Erceg E, Burns S, Roberts C, Hamilton G (2012) 'The Friendly Schools Friendly Families programme: three-year bullying behaviour outcomes in primary school children', *International Journal of Educational Research*, 53:394–406.

Design Council (2022) *Design out crime*, Design Council website, accessed 1 February 2023. https://www.designcouncil.org.uk/our-work/skills-learning/resources/design-out-crime/

Egli N, Vettenburg N, Savoie J, Lucia S, Gavray C, Zeman K (2010) 'Belgium, Canada and Switzerland: are there differences in the contributions of selected variables on self-reported property-related and violent delinquency?' *European Journal on Criminal Policy and Research*, 16(3):145–166.

Eliot M, Cornell D, Gregory A, Fan X (2010) 'Supportive school climate and student willingness to seek help for bullying and threats of violence', *Journal of School Psychology* 48(6):533–553.

Ellis J (2002) 'The importance of attending to children and place', *International Journal of Educational Policy, Research, and Practice*, 3(3):69–88.

Ellis J (2004) 'Researching children's place and space', *JCT*, 20(1):83.

eSafety Commissioner (n.d.) *eSafety* [website], accessed 1 February 2023. https://www.esafety.gov.au/

Evans GW (2003) 'The built environment and mental health', *Journal of Urban Health: Bulletin of the New York Academy of Medicine*, 80(4).

Fite PJ, Williford A, Cooley JL, DePaolis K, Rubens SL, Vernberg EM (2013) 'Patterns of victimization locations in elementary school children: effects of grade level and gender', *Child & Youth Care Forum*; 42(6):585–597.

Fram SM, Dickmann EM (2012) 'How the school built environment exacerbates bullying and peer harassment', *Children Youth and Environments*, 22(1):227–249.

Francis J, Strobel N, Trapp G, Pearce N, Vaz S, Christian H (2022) 'How does the school built environment impact students' bullying behaviour? A scoping review', *Social Science & Medicine*, 115451.

Gandini L (1993) 'Fundamentals of the Reggio Emilia approach to early childhood education', *Young Children*, 49(1):4–8.

Horton P, Forsberg C, Thornberg R (2020) '"It's hard to be everywhere": teachers' perspectives on spatiality, school design and school bullying', *International Journal of Emotional Education*, 12(2):41–55.

Hoyle JR (1977) 'Organizational and spatial characteristics of urban learning environments', *Journal of Educational Administration*, 15(1):124–132.

James SE, Herman JL, Rankin S, Keisling M, Mottet L, Anafi M (2015) *The report of the 2015 U.S. transgender survey*, National Center for Transgender Equality, Washington, DC.

Johnson SL (2009) 'Improving the school environment to reduce school violence: a review of the literature', *Journal of School Health*, 79(10):451–465.

Killeen JP, Evans GW, Danko S (2003) 'The role of permanent student artwork in students' sense of ownership in an elementary school', *Environment and Behavior*, 35(2):250–263.

Lackney JA (1999) 'Assessing school facilities for learning/assessing the impact of the physical environment on the educational process: integrating theoretical issues with practical concerns' [conference presentation], *CEFPI Northeast Chapter First Annual Conference*.

Lake EK (2014) *Conflict and playmaking: the impact of a recess enhancement program on elementary school playgrounds in New York City*, City University of New York, New York.

Langhout RD (2003) 'Reconceptualizing quantitative and qualitative methods: a case study dealing with place as an exemplar', *American Journal of Community Psychology*, 32(3):229–244.

Learning Through Landscapes (2003) *National school grounds survey: 2003*, Learning Through Landscapes, Winchester.

Malone K, Tranter P (2003) 'Children's environmental learning and the use, design and management of schoolgrounds', *Children Youth and Environments*, 13(2):87–137.

Migliaccio T, Raskauskas J, Schmidtlein M (2017) 'Mapping the landscapes of bullying', *Learning Environments Research*, 20(3):365–382.

Mulryan-Kyne C (2014) 'The school playground experience: opportunities and challenges for children and school staff', *Educational Studies*, 40(4):377–395.

Murchison GR, Agénor M, Reisner SL, Watson RJ (2019) 'School restroom and locker room restrictions and sexual assault risk among transgender youth', *Pediatrics*, 143(6):e20182902.

Porta CM, Gower AL, Mehus CJ, Yu X, Saewyc EM, Eisenberg ME (2017) '"Kicked out": LGBTQ youths' bathroom experiences and preferences', *J Adolesc*, 56:107–112.

Psychology Today (2022) *Broken Windows Theory*, Psychology Today website, accessed 1 February 2023. https://www.psychologytoday.com/us/basics/broken-windows-theory

Renalds A, Smith TH, Hale PJ (2010) 'A systematic review of built environment and health', *Family & Community Health*, 33:68–78.

Vaillancourt T, Brittain H, Bennett L, Arnocky S, McDougall P, Hymel S, Short K, Sunderani S, Scott C, Mackenzie M, Cunningham L (2010) 'Places to avoid: population-based study of student reports of unsafe and high bullying areas at school', *Canadian Journal of School Psychology*, 25(1):40–54.

Waters S, Cross D, Shaw T (2010) 'Does the nature of schools matter? An exploration of selected school ecology factors on adolescent perceptions of school connectedness', *British Journal of Educational Psychology*, 80(3):381–402.

White R (2004) *Interaction with nature during the middle years: its importance to children's development & nature's future*, White Hutchinson Leisure & Learning Group, Kansas City, MO.

WHO (World Health Organization) (2004) *The physical school environment: an essential component of a health-promoting school*, World Health Organization, Geneva.

Wilcox P, Augustine MC, Clayton RR (2006) 'Physical environment and crime and misconduct in Kentucky schools', *Journal of Primary Prevention*, 27(3):293–313.

Part 3

What's next?

Steps to effectively implement wellbeing actions needed to respond to staff and student strengths and needs

CHAPTER 8

Reviewing and renewing school wellbeing: pathways to make it happen

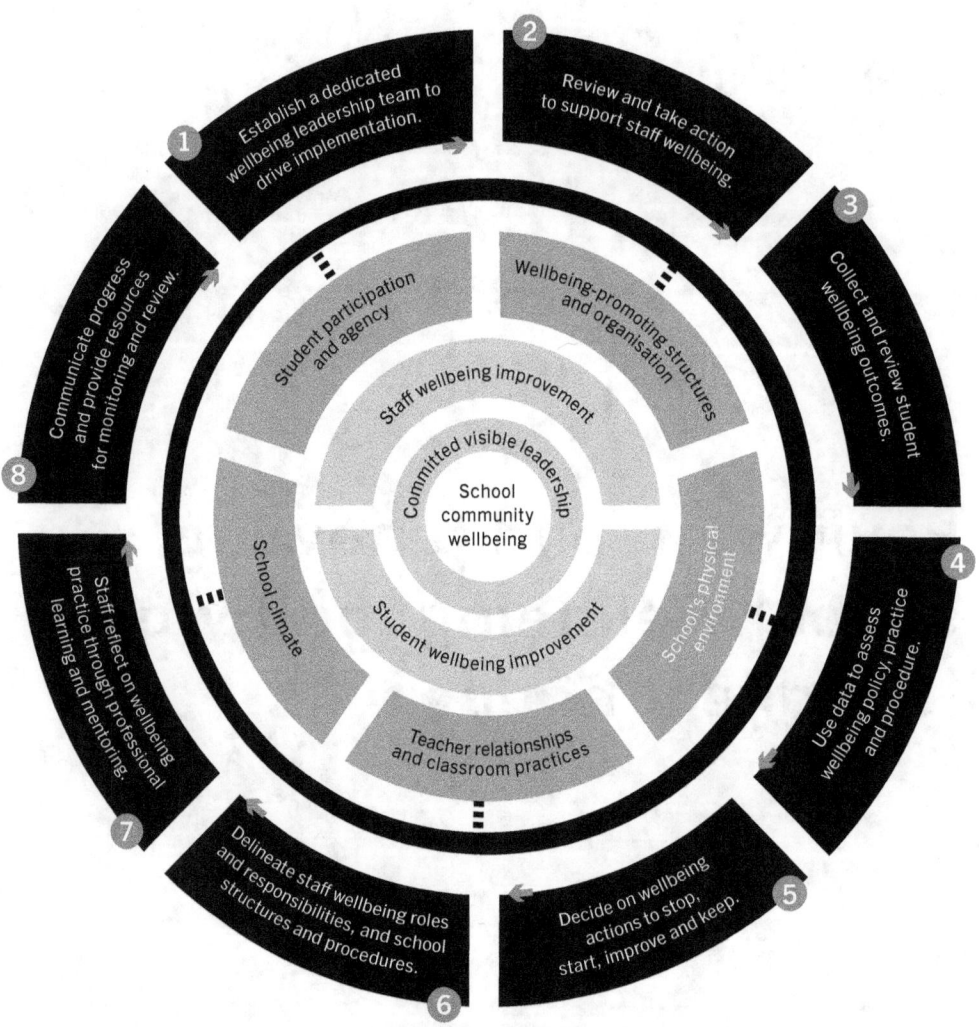

Figure 8.1. Pathways to review and renew school wellbeing

Good intentions on the part of school leaders, while essential, are not sufficient to optimise student and staff wellbeing. High-impact wellbeing leadership is visible, intentional, consistent, inclusive, responsive and sustained, and caters for the whole school community (Smith and Gowing 2021). Caring and compassionate leadership, in partnership with other leadership qualities, is fundamental to enabling caring individual relationships within a school community (Louis et al. 2016), as is the school leader's commitment to a shared vision for democratic decision-making, inclusivity and effective transparent communications.

Yet, even with a leadership mindset for wellbeing, mechanisms to address wellbeing strategically and systematically and embedded within school policies, practices, culture and resourcing can be elusive. For many schools, approaches to address wellbeing are haphazard, ad hoc and opportunistic and therefore are fragmented and not sustained. Wellbeing practices are also often not strategically connected to current practices or selected using evidence to address the specific needs of students and staff (ASPA 2008). School staff often have access to resources to improve student and staff wellbeing but lack the motivation (the will) and capacity (the skill) to effectively implement and sustain these policies and practices to benefit the whole school community (Gonzalez et al. 2020).

Like the science associated with the implementation of interventions in schools, school communities' understandings of wellbeing policy and practices and how these can be effectively implemented in schools have changed significantly over the past 20 years (Meyers 2019; Lyon and Bruns 2019).

A systematic review (Pearce et al. 2019) described the following as the most critical factors associated with the effective implementation of student wellbeing policy and practice in schools, especially when staff and student wellbeing data are used to drive decision-making:

> Take a whole-school approach.

> Focus on implementing evidence-based policies and practices.

> Establish a dedicated wellbeing leadership team to drive implementation.

> Assess staff capacity early, and boost if necessary, to enhance implementation outcomes.

> Ensure families are aware of what the school is doing and engage them meaningfully with the implementation process.

A whole-school approach is key to the effective implementation and impact of wellbeing policies and practices

As the chapters in this book demonstrate, wellbeing is most effectively enhanced through student and staff exposure to multiple levels of a school's ecology; improving student wellbeing is much more than a 'health education and personal development' curriculum.

A whole-school approach is about embedding wellbeing into the school's vision, mission, ethos, values and school improvement planning processes, to ensure it permeates the school culture and all levels of school activity – it is everyone's business. The following are typically the key components of a whole-school approach:

> leadership and commitment

> social environment (e.g. school climate, positive relationships)

> school procedures and organisation, including policies

> physical environment

> teaching and learning

> families and supportive community partnerships.

Next to families, schools are the most likely place, and for some students the only place, where they can experience the environmental conditions and learn the social, emotional and academic skills that improve their wellbeing. A whole-school approach is necessary to achieve this, as it builds a strong sense of community, helping students to feel they belong in and are connected to the school – especially when each student has a positive relationship with at least one capable and caring adult in the school.

Common understandings and responsibility for whole-school wellbeing policies and practices are maximised when these are co-developed with staff, students and parents. Co-development increases relevancy and builds ownership, which in turn strengthens the school climate. It also increases clarity within the school community about wellbeing organisation and structures, and wellbeing roles and responsibilities and importantly, it helps to strengthen relationships with families. This shared understanding and collective whole-school responsibility for wellbeing also enhances the implementation (the school community's exposure to activities), and therefore the impact and sustainability, of wellbeing policies and practices (Gonzalez 2020).

Additionally, a whole-school approach drives the consistent delivery of positive processes for wellbeing and their 'fit' with the school climate. It helps to increase the 'skill' and the 'will' of staff to implement and sustain the wellbeing policies and practices they have co-developed (Sancassiani et al. 2015). As discussed below, whole-school representation in the wellbeing leadership team, including the voices of diverse students and families, is a critical part of this process.

Implementation using a whole-school approach also considers the full spectrum of policies and practices school staff can implement to optimise student social and emotional wellbeing. This spectrum of policies and practices includes:

> universal whole-school promotion, protection and prevention activities embedded in school systems and processes (including teaching and learning) to improve the wellbeing of all students

> targeted actions to support students with special needs or those who are at higher risk of wellbeing problems, by strengthening the ability of students to identify, assess and manage issues

> intensive individual casework to provide immediate support (including helping students to access external community care, treatment or counselling services) to reduce the intensity, severity and duration of their risk behaviour and to support their reintegration to school.

Quality meta-analyses data show that 'targeted practices', such as counselling services for students at risk of behavioural or emotional problems, are more effective (especially for social and emotional adjustment outcomes) than more generalised support (Goldberg et al. 2019). Hence, appropriate training and support in targeted practices, such as trauma-informed practices, are needed for teachers and other staff who are helping higher risk students. As discussed later, whole-school staff professional learning is also needed to help staff adopt and embed teaching practices that promote academic care and support students' learning and practice of social and emotional skills.

To monitor the implementation of all these co-designed, high-impact, whole-school wellbeing policies and practices, school leaders need to have processes in place to understand if students feel:

> ❯ safe (culturally, physically, emotionally and socially safe and treated fairly and equitably)

> ❯ challenged (supported with high expectations and strong motivation, school activities connected to student life goals, quality academic opportunities)

> ❯ socially capable (cooperative, responsible and persistent, emotionally competent, empowered and with opportunities to contribute to the school community, such as through peer support or leadership)

> ❯ supported (strong sense of belonging to the school, positive relationships with staff and students, consistently effective and available support).

This chapter provides an implementation framework and recommendations to help school leaders support their wellbeing leadership teams to maximise staff implementation of quality evidence-based wellbeing policies, practices, procedures and professional development.

Planning to effectively implement evidence-based whole-school wellbeing policy and practice

While all school leaders are expected to adhere to national and state government and institutional wellbeing-related directives, such as the *Melbourne declaration on educational goals for young Australians* (Ministerial Council on Education, Employment, Training and Youth Affairs Melbourne 2008), the Australian Curriculum's *Personal and Social Capabilities* (ACARA 2019) and the *Australian Student Wellbeing Framework* and Wellbeing Hub (ESA 2018), none of these resources provide clear implementation processes for school wellbeing improvement review and planning. Yet, implementation failure of evidence-based resources is one of the most common factors limiting the effectiveness of wellbeing interventions.

The major factors that contribute to implementation failure include poor wellbeing leadership, inattention to whether the school community is ready and insufficient resources and staff capacity and motivation to effectively implement the evidence-based actions with fidelity.

A strategic implementation process led by the wellbeing leadership team helps them to work purposefully to avoid the problems of 'programitis', where school staff may feel compelled to take on new innovations without due consideration of:

> the quality of evidence that informed the wellbeing resource's development

> the resource's suitability for the school context, particularly student needs

> where these fit within the current suite of school wellbeing effort

> staff training needed for effective implementation.

Wellbeing needs to be integrated into the whole-school social and physical environment, the curriculum, the pedagogy, policies, procedures and structures at the school and partnerships inherent within and outside the school, by school staff, students, their families and community groups.

A strategic wellbeing implementation process must be planned and orchestrated by the wellbeing leadership team while meaningfully engaging the whole school via thoughtful planning, sustained attention and review, collaboration and meaningful resourcing.

Using the critical implementation factors (Pearce et al. 2022) associated with the effective implementation of student wellbeing policy and practice in schools described above, the 8-step implementation process (see the outer ring of Figure 8.1 at the beginning of this chapter) will guide school leaders and their wellbeing leadership team's review, planning and implementation processes for staff and student wellbeing improvement.

Step 1: Establish a dedicated wellbeing leadership team to drive implementation

Given creating and sustaining change is challenging in complex school environments, especially when addressing wellbeing at a whole-school level, school leaders need to establish and provide sustained support for a wellbeing leadership team, including building their capacity. As discussed in Chapter 6, a dedicated wellbeing team is necessary, as a single wellbeing staff champion can quickly burn out working alone in this role.

The school wellbeing leadership team has responsibility for driving the planning, motivating, resourcing, monitoring, evaluating and encouraging the school community's delivery of the full spectrum of wellbeing policy and practice actions. Part 2 of this book, 'What's needed?' (Chapters 3–7), suggests multiple high-impact policy and practice pathways to improve student and staff wellbeing. These policy and practice actions are related and mutually supporting but are also sufficiently discrete to be considered separately. The more policy and practice actions accessed by students and staff, the better their wellbeing.

Planning by the wellbeing team will ensure the implementation of these wellbeing actions is a coordinated process, not an event, where policies and practices are integrated and not competing, and where the impact is equitable for all students' wellbeing. Ad hoc or fragmented implementation can affect student engagement and staff morale (Elias 2009).

Step 2: Review and take action to support staff wellbeing

Given the very strong link between staff wellbeing and student wellbeing, it is essential for the staff wellbeing team to consider the wellbeing status of their school's staff when addressing the wellbeing of students.

Staff wellbeing is influenced by caring and supportive relationships within the school community, which in turn affects staff relationships with other staff and students (Cefai and Cavioni 2013). When staff feel well and cared for, they are more likely to see the benefit of and be engaged in optimising student wellbeing. Chapter 1 provides examples of policies and practices that can be implemented to help audit, assess, act on and monitor staff wellbeing.

Staff readiness to support students' wellbeing also needs to be considered in the context of their overall wellbeing. Increasing evidence indicates how important it is to assess staff readiness for implementation, such as understanding their capacity needs (see Step 7) to ensure successful implementation (Kingston et al. 2018). Student, parent and staff satisfaction surveys and exit interviews are another source of data that can provide some insight into how the school community is feeling.

Step 3: Collect and review student wellbeing outcomes

Part 1 of this book, 'What's Happening?'(Chapters 1 and 2), suggests that a fundamental high-impact practice for school leaders is to understand and regularly monitor and evaluate student (and staff) wellbeing outcomes. This knowledge helps school leaders to use limited resources more efficiently and effectively and helps them drive and respond to the school community's wellbeing capacity, interests, strengths, needs, threats and opportunities.

Further, a comprehensive understanding of the school context and the community's unique culture is critical to the successful implementation of wellbeing initiatives. Chapter 2 describes processes and tools to help schools routinely collect different types of student wellbeing data that increases staff understanding of student wellbeing and opportunities for improvement.

Data already collected by the school that typically correlate with student wellbeing include measures of academic achievement, behaviour and attendance. Some school leaders supplement these data with qualitative or standardised quantitative wellbeing survey tools that assess specific student wellbeing outcomes, such as autonomy, belonging, competence, emotional regulation, peer support and school engagement. These tools (examples are provided in Chapter 2) can assess the wellbeing strengths, needs and interests of students and help the school staff to understand the impact of its wellbeing initiatives.

These data can also help school leadership teams to strategically identify, benchmark and monitor the student wellbeing outcomes to be targeted by the school. Chapter 2 describes the strategic value of assessing students' wellbeing to guide decision-making. It also shows how schools' routine data sets and tools could be used to assess and respond to student wellbeing.

When staff can see the wellbeing strengths and needs of their own students and are invited to contribute to the school's response, they are more amenable to supporting and implementing the associated policies, procedures and practices.

Step 4: Use data to assess wellbeing policy, practice and procedure

Most schools are very engaged in implementing multiple policies, procedures, practices and professional learning to address student (and staff) wellbeing. However, these actions are often isolated (at a teacher level or year level) rather than a coordinated component of an overall improvement plan for wellbeing. As a result, the staff implementing (and the students receiving) these policies and practices may not realise the synergistic value of the school's overall wellbeing effort.

As mentioned in Step 1, the wellbeing leadership team plays a critical role as the conductor and harmoniser of the 'orchestra of wellbeing effort' in the school. Importantly, this team needs to:

> comprehensively understand, coordinate and support the school's 'wellbeing effort' to maximise its effectiveness

> audit what wellbeing-related policies, procedures, practices and professional learning (capacity building) are being offered, where and to whom (e.g. Year 7 only) and under what circumstances (e.g. as a targeted intervention for higher risk students)

> determine what policies, procedures, practices and professional learning are worth keeping, what's promising but needs improving, what needs to be cut and what's missing.

To understand the school wellbeing effort, the wellbeing leadership team needs to engage key staff (or, if possible, the whole school community) in the process of mapping the current policies, procedures, practices and professional learning the school currently has in train to address wellbeing. The team also needs sufficient resources and time to effectively conduct this wellbeing effort audit process.

Findings from a systematic and regular wellbeing audit and mapping process help the wellbeing leadership team to cultivate and sustain insight into all the school is doing to address wellbeing and to inform their decision-making to improve this effort (see Table 8.1

for example questions to consider for this school-level wellbeing effort audit and mapping process).

Table 8.1. Sample questions for mapping and auditing a school's wellbeing effort

MAPPING CURRENT WELLBEING POLICIES, PRACTICES AND PROFESSIONAL LEARNING				
Questions	Year level			
	Foundation	Year 1	Year 2	Year 3 etc.
What are the school's current actions? Examples: • curriculum • pedagogy • policy • social environment • physical environment procedures/ structures (e.g. homeroom) • parent and community partnerships				
What level of support is provided by this activity? Examples: • universal support • support for students at risk • support for students experiencing difficulties				
What wellbeing SEL outcomes or school strategy outcomes are addressed?				
What's promising but needs to be improved and how?				
What's working well and needs to be maintained?				
What new actions are needed?				
What needs to stop?				

By mapping the school's wellbeing effort, the wellbeing leadership team can:

> document and understand current whole-school (including classroom) policies and practices that address:

- the promotion of student wellbeing and prevention of wellbeing difficulties (e.g. whole-school, universal actions). This includes a review by staff of key learning areas and an audit of relevant curricular scope and sequence
- students who are at higher risk of wellbeing difficulties (e.g. early intervention)
- students who are currently experiencing difficulties (e.g. case management and treatment)

> determine how these evidence-based policies and practices contribute to a whole-school strategy to equitably address student wellbeing

> identify strengths, overlaps and gaps in the school's policies and practices and the staff driving or given responsibility for these actions (e.g. early childhood teaching staff are responsible for Paths Social Emotional Learning curriculum; dean of students drives the Be You resources, addressing school culture); consider the appropriateness and effectiveness of current policies, practices and professional learning and the extent to which these actions address (or with further support, will address) the identified student wellbeing needs in Step 3

> use scarce wellbeing resources more effectively by identifying and implementing economies of scale and effort

> make recommendations for future action to improve student wellbeing (see Step 5).

Lastly, it is important for current school wellbeing policies, procedures, practices and professional learning to be mapped against the student outcome data collected in Step 3 and for the school's strategic or operational plan to determine their usefulness, relevance and compatibility with school community needs. For example, if the student data suggest that a particular area of wellbeing (e.g. connectedness to school) or a subset of students (such as year 11 and 12 female students) are showing higher levels of anxiety, the school can assess what actions are being taken to address these issues or target this subgroup using this evidence and adjust the school's wellbeing resource allocation accordingly, as shown in Step 5.

Step 5: Decide on wellbeing actions to stop, start, improve and keep

Information from Step 4 helps the wellbeing leadership team to use student outcome data and the mapped school wellbeing effort data to assess the relative contribution of components of their school's wellbeing effort and decide how to improve current action and staff implementation to optimise student and staff wellbeing.

Given wellbeing policies and practices do not equally improve wellbeing (i.e. some are more effective than others), the wellbeing leadership team also need to use quality research (along with their practice-based evidence) to determine the impact of policies, practices, procedures and professional learning that are currently being implemented and those they are considering for implementation. For example, the large MYRIAD study conducted in the UK in 2022 found that mindfulness programs for students in their early teens were not effective for improving student wellbeing and that some may even be counterproductive (Montero-Marin et al. 2022).

The wellbeing implementation team need to use evidence of factors that predict the effectiveness of school wellbeing policies and practices to decide and plan what actions need to be kept, stopped, redirected and improved (and when and for which groups) as well as to determine what's missing. Factors include the type of practice (e.g. SEL curriculum delivery) and the way it is best implemented and sustained and the school's own available student evidence. The wellbeing leadership team can use this step in the implementation process to identify what wellbeing actions are making a difference or where there is an unfulfilled need, and adjust the resource allocations to achieve the best wellbeing outcomes.

The team also needs to consider the necessary 'dose' and mix of practices needed to have a positive effect on student wellbeing outcomes. For example, one-off guest speaker visits to a school to address wellbeing, while possibly a trigger for action, do not provide sufficient dose to improve and sustain student wellbeing outcomes. The guest speaker may provide better value to the school delivering professional development to staff, than presenting for a limited time to students.

Decision-making about the relative contribution of wellbeing actions needs to be a collaborative process led by the wellbeing leadership team. Determination by staff and other members of the school community (including students) as to which wellbeing policies, procedures and practices are currently working well to address student wellbeing is an important step.

As mentioned in Chapter 5, amplifying student voice in this decision-making process is also important, especially given their increased need for autonomy as they age (Shinde et al. 2020). Similarly, meaningful engagement with diverse families to seek their input (as discussed in Step 8 further on) also helps to enhance community ownership and support for the implementation of recommended wellbeing policies and practices.

To maximise their implementation of wellbeing actions, teachers, including specialist or non-teaching staff such as the school counsellor, also need to provide input into deciding which actions will be implemented. Teachers have expert knowledge about their students' needs and strengths. Additionally, as described in Step 7, school staff need professional learning to support their implementation of practices, to match their context and students' needs and to integrate these into their daily work pattern.

While identifying evidence-based policies, practices, procedures and professional learning is essential, it is insufficient to maximise the effectiveness of wellbeing actions. To be effective, wellbeing actions must also be implemented well (Durlak et al. 2011) by motivated school staff who have capacity and who understand their roles and responsibilities, as described in Step 6.

Step 6: Delineate staff wellbeing roles and responsibilities, and school structures and procedures

As described in Chapter 6, staff clarity about their student wellbeing roles and responsibilities and having school structures and procedures to support them in this role breeds commitment. This includes staff feeling committed to the school's wellbeing vision and feeling confident about their contribution to its implementation. Wellbeing initiatives are effective when 'everyone in the school community knows, and feels secure in the knowledge, that as valued members of that community they can participate in giving and receiving encouragement, guidance and support' (Clemett and Pearce 1989:16).

Step 6 is necessary to help staff understand their roles, responsibilities and contribution to improving the wellbeing of students at a whole-school level, in addition to their classroom teaching and pedagogy. It also promotes an understanding of the importance of wellbeing across the whole school community and identifies potential capacity needs to connect with support beyond the school.

The Australian government's guiding principles for a safe and supportive environment states that Australian schools must ensure that roles and responsibilities of all members of the school community in promoting a safe and supportive environment are explicit, clearly understood and disseminated (Commonwealth Department of Australia 2005).

Clearly delineating staff wellbeing roles and responsibilities and connecting these to staff job descriptions, role purpose and key duties can challenge busy staff and crowded curricula, especially given teachers report difficulties in trying to balance supporting student wellbeing with other academic demands (Willis et al. 2019). Hence the need, as discussed in Step 7, to build staff motivation, self-efficacy and capacity to improve student wellbeing and to consistently acknowledge, support and reward the quality implementation of wellbeing actions by staff.

Step 7: Staff reflect on wellbeing practice through professional learning and mentoring

As teachers' relationships with students, their pedagogy (including their classroom management style) and the social climate they establish with students can impact student wellbeing, the wellbeing leadership team need to prioritise professional learning, mentoring and communities of practice to build staff motivation, confidence and capacity to support student wellbeing (see Chapter 4 for more information).

During the wellbeing policies and practices audit and mapping process described in Step 4, the wellbeing leadership team are encouraged to assess staff readiness and capacity ('the skill') to implement the school's wellbeing effort. This can be conducted with a sample of staff or by asking all staff to self-assess their capacity using tools such as those developed by Cefai and Cavioni (2013). With this insight, meaningful whole-school professional learning or other modes of capacity-building needs and interests may be identified to improve staff implementation of actions to promote student wellbeing.

Some staff may need encouragement to actively participate in professional learning related to student wellbeing, rather than specific to their learning area, especially in secondary schools. Consequently, capacity building needs to motivate staff ('the will') by building their understanding that their academic care, student wellbeing support roles, how they teach and organise their classrooms, their relationships with students, and the social and learning environment they create can significantly enhance or harm the wellbeing of students (and their own wellbeing) and improve their students' behaviour and academic outcomes (Nadge 2005).

Staff who can see the relevance and importance of wellbeing practices are more likely to take them seriously, participate in professional learning and implement them appropriately (Shinde et al. 2020). Addressing 'why' wellbeing is important also helps staff to genuinely understand:

> the relevance and importance of addressing student (and staff) wellbeing

> how improving student (and staff) wellbeing will directly and indirectly (e.g. through better student engagement) improve students' academic achievement

> the importance of building the cultural competence of school staff to ensure they recognise the significance and impact of the school community's cultural backgrounds on students' wellbeing.

Much evidence shows that quality professional learning via workshops, teacher-to-teacher observation and regular booster sessions is essential to improve staff implementation of whole-school and classroom wellbeing actions (Durlak et al. 2011; Fenwick-Smith et al. 2018). Horizontal knowledge transfer between school staff, such as by shadowing other teachers implementing practices, also helps to build communities of practice among the staff and improves or removes poor practices, while embedding effective practices. This training must ideally involve the whole school staff, but at a minimum, the schools' wellbeing leaders, classroom teachers of social and emotional learning and homeroom staff.

Step 8: Communicate progress and provide resources for monitoring and review

It is critical that the school community – staff, students and their families – deeply understands the rationale, goals, actions and subsequent outcomes of its whole-school wellbeing strategy and actions. Family understanding and involvement is key to the success of any measure directed towards enhancing the wellbeing of children.

From the outset of the wellbeing improvement planning process, leaders need to keep their school community regularly informed about the actions the wellbeing team are taking to improve student and staff wellbeing, and the outcomes of these actions. In the early stage of this communication process, leaders may also consider presenting how the recommendations and actions were determined, how the vision, mission and strategic plan of the school are being supported by the wellbeing policies and how they are operationalised by the wellbeing practices and procedures. These brief communications to the whole school community need to happen early and should be updated often, including, for example, a standing item at staff, student leader and parent and carer meetings, with presentations of important findings and next steps, as appropriate, to the school community.

Communicating about wellbeing improvement often begins with 'why' – explaining why it is important for a school's unique context to address student wellbeing and the impact it will have on students' health, social and emotional development and learning. It may also be useful to explain why addressing wellbeing can improve teachers' effectiveness, enjoyment of teaching, relationships with students and overall health. Additionally, the leadership team may decide to share some of the aggregated student wellbeing data collected by the school to help the community understand students' general wellbeing strengths, needs and interests.

To help build the school's wellbeing improvement momentum, it is necessary to ensure ongoing communication and other engagement with the full diversity of school community to capture their genuine interest, recommendations and support for the improvement activities (for example, being mindful of the need to translate or support communications to families whose first language isn't English). Leaders of the wellbeing team may also consider sharing community recommendations with the school community, or at least the process followed to collect this insight and determine the recommended actions.

The second major stage of communicating progress needs to address the 'what'; what policy, practices and procedure recommendations are being implemented, and by when. Leaders may consider describing aspects of the school's continuum of care, ranging from whole-school universal wellbeing promotion activities (such as creating a positive and engaged school culture and community) to targeted prevention (such as the explicit teaching of social and emotional skills) and individual intervention or support of students experiencing difficulties (often delivered by the allied health professionals in the community).

Communication also needs to include the 'how'; how these wellbeing improvement actions are being resourced and how they can be sustained. This includes, where needed, communicating how support will be provided for the development of wellbeing knowledge and understanding, and skill building for staff, students and families. This communication will help to ensure a consistency of approach and appropriate fit with school culture, encouraging better community understanding and increasing the likelihood of the adoption and maintenance of the recommended wellbeing actions.

Finally, as part of this ongoing wellbeing communication process, it will be important for leaders to feed back the impact of, or outcomes from, their wellbeing activities to the school community, as the wellbeing team monitor the progress of the recommended actions taken. Regularly sharing progress of the impact of policies, practices and procedures with staff, students, families and the wider community is needed. This may also mean identifying 'quick wins' to demonstrate progress to the school community. As discussed in Chapter 7, changes to the physical environment, such as availability of sports equipment and active teacher supervision in hotspot areas in the school, can often contribute to immediate positive change with a limited investment in time and other resources.

Concluding thoughts for leaders

One of the most important priorities for schools is to grow the 'whole' student, so that they become socially, emotionally, physically and morally competent adults. While cognitive outcomes are important, students are under-served if this is the only priority outcome in schools. Significant and robust national and international evidence shows that school systems and leaders must help to develop students holistically, rather than focus only on actions that improve students' academic competence (Green and Norrish 2013; OECD 2015).

Interestingly, research reports that gaps in student achievement may be best addressed by tackling the students' social and emotional wellbeing skills gap, rather than by intensifying cognitive instruction alone. MacCann et al.'s (2020) meta-analysis found that a student's academic achievement was strongly predicted by their emotional intelligence (emotional regulation skills, social skills and self-motivational capacity). Heckman et al. (2006) also report that 'non-cognitive ability' (i.e. social and emotional skills) is as important, if not more important, than cognitive ability when considering key later life outcomes, such as secondary school completion, secondary school final marks, tertiary participation and broader life issues like finding a life partner and earning a good wage for one's labour.

Addressing wellbeing is a school's everyday business and everyone's business. It should not be represented only through haphazard responses, as occurred in some schools during the COVID-19 pandemic. School leaders have an opportunity to fulfill the vision of the *Australian Student Wellbeing Framework*: 'promoting student wellbeing, providing a safe and connected setting marked by positive relationships, to ensure students achieve their fullest potential' (ESA 2018).

While numerous Australian policies, such as the *Australian Student Wellbeing Framework*, promote the need to support school leaders' decision-making about ways to improve student and staff wellbeing, these provide almost no support or resources to help school staff assess what evidence-based action they need to take – in accordance with their own context and students' (and staff's) wellbeing strengths and needs. This insight is needed to prioritise, select, successfully implement and embed wellbeing actions in the school to maximise their effectiveness.

While it can be challenging for school wellbeing leaders to prioritise the implementation of a strategic wellbeing improvement plan, without a genuine commitment from the school leader to involve and transform their whole school into a learning community that prioritises wellbeing, the effectiveness of actions to improve student wellbeing and associated student engagement and academic achievement will be significantly diminished.

To build wellbeing-focused momentum and to ensure the ongoing engagement, implementation and sustainability of the school's wellbeing effort, appointing a wellbeing leadership team is essential. This team needs to be actively supported by the school leader and provided sufficient resources, capability and time to lead. The team also needs opportunities to assess student and staff need, co-develop, disseminate, monitor and communicate a short- and longer term wellbeing improvement plan – prioritised within and yoked to the school strategic and master planning process.

Effective school leaders, along with their wellbeing leadership team, understand that the audit, review and collection of school-level data is critical to understand and respond to the status of staff and student wellbeing. These data help to determine, in consultation with the school community, what is working well, what's needed and how to implement and sustain key wellbeing policies and practices.

While there is no silver bullet for enhancing a school's approach to improving its community's wellbeing, all actions must be implemented well and sustained to make a difference for students. As this book has argued, a master wellbeing improvement plan is not a 'nice to have'; it is an essential pre-requisite for students' academic achievement.

Quality school leadership is one of the most important predictors of student and staff wellbeing. School leaders have a responsibility to ensure the 15,000 hours students spend at school, from early childhood to late adolescence, comprise high-impact actions that evidence shows can have a significant effect on students' wellbeing (as well as that of leaders and staff) and associated academic achievement and behaviour.

References

ACARA (Australian Curriculum Assessment and Reporting Authority) (2019) *Personal and Social Capability (Version 8.4)*, ACARA website, accessed 17 January 2023. https://www.australiancurriculum.edu.au/f-10-curriculum/general-capabilities/personal-and-social-capability/

ASPA (2008) *Policy position statement: student wellbeing,* accessed 17 January 2023. http://www.aspa.asn.au.

Cefai C, Cavioni V (2013) *Social and emotional education in primary school: integrating theory and research into practice*, Springer, New York.

Clemett AJ, Pearce JS (1989) *The evaluation of pastoral care*, Blackwell, Oxford.

Commonwealth Department of Australia (2005), *Report on the National Safe Schools Framework best practice grants programmes (2004–2005)*, Australian Government Department of Education, Science and Training, Canberra.

Durlak JA, Weissberg RP, Dymnicki AB, Taylor RD, Schellinger KB (2011) 'The impact of enhancing students' social and emotional learning: a meta-analysis of school-based universal interventions', *Child Development*, 82(1):405–432.

Elias MJ (2009) 'Social–emotional and character development and academics as a dual focus of educational policy', *Educational Policy*, 23(6):831–846.

ESA (Education Services Australia) (2018) *Australian Student Wellbeing Framework*, Education Council, Carlton South, VIC, accessed 17 January 2023. https://studentwellbeinghub.edu.au/educators/framework

Fenwick-Smith A, Dahlberg EE, Thompson SC (2018) 'Systematic review of resilience-enhancing, universal, primary school-based mental health promotion programs', *BMC Psychology*, 6(1):1–17.

Goldberg JM, Sklad M, Elfrink TR, KMG Schreurs, ET Bohlmeijer, Clarke AM (2019) 'Effectiveness of interventions adopting a whole school approach to enhancing social and emotional development: a meta-analysis', *European Journal of Psychology of Education*, 34(4):755–782.

Gonzalez GC, Cerully JL, Wang EL, Schweig J, Todd I, Johnston WR, J Schnittka (2020) *Social and emotional learning, school climate, and school safety: a randomized-controlled trial evaluation of tools for life® in elementary and middle schools*, research report. RR-4285-NIJ, RAND Corporation.

Green LS, Norrish JM (2013) 'Enhancing well-being in adolescents: positive psychology and coaching psychology interventions in schools', in Proctor C, Linley PA (eds) *Research, applications, and interventions for children and adolescents*, Springer, Dordrecht.

Heckman JJ, Stixrud J, Urzua S (2006) 'The effects of cognitive and noncognitive abilities on labor market outcomes and social behavior', *Journal of Labor Economics*, 24(3):411–482.

Kingston B, Mattson SA, Dymnicki A, Spier E, Fitzgerald M, Shipman K, Goodrum S, Woodward W, Witt J, Hill KG, Elliott D (2018) 'Building schools' readiness to implement a comprehensive approach to school safety', *Clinical Child and Family Psychology Review*, 21(4):433–449.

Louis KS, Murphy J, Smylie M (2016) 'Caring leadership in schools: Findings from exploratory analyses', *Educational Administration Quarterly*, 52(2):310–348.

Lyon AR, Bruns EJ (2019) 'From evidence to impact: joining our best school mental health practices with our best implementation strategies', *School Mental Health*, 11(1):106–114.

MacCann C, Jiang Y, Brown LER, Double KS, Bucich M, Minbashian A (2020) 'Emotional intelligence predicts academic performance: a meta-analysis', *Psychological Bulletin*, 146(2):150–186.

Mertens E, Deković M, Leijten P, Van Londen M, Reitz E (2020) 'Components of school-based interventions stimulating students' intrapersonal and interpersonal domains: a meta-analysis', *Clinical Child and Family Psychology Review*, 23:605–631.

Meyers DC (2019) 'Supporting systemic social and emotional learning with a schoolwide implementation model', *Evaluation and Program Planning*, 73:53–61.

Ministerial Council on Education, Employment, Training and Youth Affairs (2008) *Melbourne declaration on educational goals for young Australians*, Ministerial Council on Education, Employment, Training and Youth Affairs, accessed 14 March 2023. http://www.curriculum.edu.au/verve/_resources/National_Declaration_on_the_Educational_Goals_for_Young_Australians.pdf

Montero-Marin J, Allwood M, Ball S, Crane C, De Wilde K, Hinze V, Jones B, Lord L, Nuthall E, Raja A, Taylor A, Tudor K, MYRIAD team, Blakemore S-J, Byford S, Dalgleish T, Ford T, Greenberg MT, Ukoumunne OC, Williams JMG, Kuyken W (2022) 'School-based mindfulness training in early adolescence: what works, for whom and how in the MYRIAD trial?' *Evidence-based Mental Health*, 25(3):117–124.

Nadge A (2005) 'Academic care: from research to reality', *Independent Education*, 35(2):30–32.

OECD (Organization for Economic Co-operation and Development) (2015) *Skills for social progress: the power of social and emotional skills*, OECD Publishing, Paris.

Pearce N, Cross D, Epstein M, Johnston R, Legge E (2019) *Strengthening school and system capacity to implement effective interventions to support student behaviour and wellbeing in NSW public schools: an evidence review*, Telethon Kids Institute, Perth, Western Australia.

Pearce N, Monks H, Alderman N, Hearn L, Burns S, Runions K, Francis J, Cross D (2022) '"It's all about context": building school capacity to implement a whole-school approach to bullying', *International Journal of Bullying Prevention*, 1–16, Advance online publication. https://doi.org/10.1007/s42380-022-00138-6

Runions K, Sae-Koew J, Pearce N, Cross D December (2022) *The state of research on bullying and intervening to reduce bullying in schools: a report for the Victorian Department of Education and Training*, Telethon Kids Institute, Perth, Western Australia.

Runions KC, Vitaro F, Cross D, Boivin M (2014) 'Teacher–child relationship, parenting, and growth in likelihood and severity of physical aggression in the early school years', *Merrill-Palmer Quarterly*, 60(3):274–301.

Sancassiani F, Pintus E, Holte A, Paulus P, Moro MF, Cossu G, Angermeyer MC, Carat MG, Lindert J (2015) 'Enhancing the emotional and social skills of the youth to promote their wellbeing and positive development: a systematic review of universal school-based randomized controlled trials', *Clinical Practice and Epidemiology in Mental Health*, 11(Suppl 1 M2):21.

Sheridan SM, Witte AL, Holmes SR, Coutts MJ, Dent AL, Kunz GM, Wu C (2012) 'A randomized trial examining the effects of conjoint behavioral consultation and the mediating role of the parent–teacher relationship', *School Psychology Review*, 41(1):23–46.

Shinde S, Khandeparkar P, Pereira B, Sharma A, Ross DA, Weiss H, Patton GC, Patel V (2020) *What makes multicomponent school-based health promotion interventions work? A qualitative study nested in the SEHER trial in Bihar, India*.

Smith C, Gowing A (2021) 'A leadership mindset for wellbeing', *Australian Educational Leader*, 43(1):54–56.

Willis A, Hyde M, Black A (2019) 'Juggling with both hands tied behind my back: teachers' views and experiences of the tensions between student well-being concerns and academic performance improvement agendas', *American Educational Research Journal*, 56(6):2644–2673.

www.ingramcontent.com/pod-product-compliance
Lightning Source LLC
Chambersburg PA
CBHW051404070526
44584CB00023B/3283